Second Edition

FAMILY TABLE SERVICE

For Today's Living

by

The late
KATHRYN BELE NILES
Former Director of Home Economics
Poultry and Egg National Board

HILDEGARDE STREUFERT
Department of Home Economics
Arizona State University

Burgess Publishing Company
Minneapolis, Minn.

Printed in the United States of America
Library of Congress Catalog Card Number 67-16364
SBN 8087-1409-0

PUBLISHER'S NOTE

Since 1930 Burgess Publishing Company has published *Family Table Service* by Kathryn B. Niles. Thousands of teachers, students, and homemakers have used this small volume to teach or learn gracious but simple ways of serving meals in the home.

Now the material has been revised and brought up to date, carrying forward the long history of the book, but focusing on the more casual and informal dining patterns of today.

Mrs. Niles is well known for her contributions to the home economics field, both as a teacher of foods and nutrition, and as the Director of Home Economics, Poultry and Egg National Board. She is an honorary lifetime member of the Institute of American Poultry and the National Turkey Federation and has been named to the Hall of Fame, American Poultry Historical Society for her work in research and consumer education. However, because Mrs. Niles has retired from actual participation in school activities, she believed a co-author, currently teaching home economics, was necessary to prepare a revised edition. Mrs. Niles has continued her professional interest as a consultant.

Hildegarde Streufert, a member of the home economics staff at Arizona State University, has long been familiar with *Family Table Service*. Her knowledge and enthusiasm about the book, and her professional qualifications, made her an ideal co-author.

After Miss Streufert completed her undergraduate work at the University of Minnesota, she taught home economics in secondary schools. She did her graduate work at Iowa State University where she received her master's degree. Miss Streufert has taught courses in clothing, textiles and related arts at Valparaiso University, Syracuse University, Oregon State University, and Arizona State University. Being an active member of several professional organizations and an author of several publications, she is aware of current trends and practices in the teaching of home economics at various levels. Her knowledge and experience are reflected in the new edition of *Family Table Service for Today's Living*.

We are very pleased and proud to continue to publish this book in a revised edition, which we expect to be as useful and successful as the original edition of 1930.

The Publisher

PREFACE

Family Table Service for Today's Living represents a complete revision and enlargement of *Family Table Service* first published in 1930. The latter was designed to fill a need for food classes in the Division of Home Economics, University of Minnesota and to provide the busy student with a simple text on the basic principles of table service.

Family Table Service for Today's Living is the very essence of its title, recognizing the changing habits of family interests and ideals. The informality of casual living does not mean dropping basic standards and principles. The well-scrubbed pine table with its earthenware or the beautifully finished dining table with its elegant appointments are undergirded with the same fundamentals of good style and taste. This revised edition is expanded by additional text material, photographs and line drawings, some in color, yet it faithfully fulfills the needs and interests of the same students and teachers who relied upon the earlier text for direction and help. A Suggested Reading list is included, and an appendix has been added which includes "A Little More about Carving Equipment and Kitchen Tools," "A Little More about Tableware," and a "Dictionary of Food, Foreign Phrases and Menu Terms."

The Authors hope that the best and most useful of the original text have been retained and that, with the addition of the new, the book will better serve students and teachers at every level of instruction, as well as others who are interested in gracious family meals.

Kathryn Bele Niles
Hildegarde Streufert

ACKNOWLEDGEMENTS

In the planning and writing of the first revision of *Family Table Service*, the authors realized the extent of change and the amazing variety in the areas which concerned them "for Today's Living." Conferences and correspondence with selected representatives supplied helpful factual information. To these people we are grateful for their counsel and assistance.

The authors gratefully acknowledge the generous and ready response of the two organizations listed below in supplying photographs and accompanying text.

The National Live Stock and Meat Board (chapter 7, pages 46-51 and page 114); and

The Poultry and Egg National Board (chapter 2, page 7, chapter 5, page 34, chapter 6, page 40, chapter 7, pages 52, 54, 59 and pages 112 and 114 in which PENB photographs are used).

Further acknowledgement is made to the following individuals at Arizona State University:

Mr. John Dutson
Photographic Service

Mr. Michael Obrenovich
Graphic Artist

Mr. Fred Krueger and
Mrs. Genevieve Brewster
Commercial Artists

TABLE OF CONTENTS

Chapter I

PLANNING FOR TABLE SERVICE

"The psychology of eating is important, and the major function of table service is to contribute to it."

Probably no other phase of family living can do more to unify the family group or bring health and happiness to its members than the fellowship enjoyed at meal time, which, for many, has become the only meeting place for family members. It is a time when tact and consideration for others, as well as friendly hospitality, are practiced. No one can deny the importance and value of courtesy and pleasing manners at the family table. It is often said the behavior of an individual at the table unconsciously betrays his social training and refinement.

Customs in table service change from year to year. For this reason no definite set of rules can be said to be either generally accepted or approved. Table customs may vary within a given time between countries or between localities of the same country. Is it for us to cling to a tradition of long standing for tradition's sake, or to adapt ourselves to modifications of customs that are perhaps more convenient and comfortable for our time and circumstances? To illustrate one break from tradition in this country, consider the fork-shifting method of eating main-course foods. It is quite different from the non-shifting method associated with Europeans. Another example of change is the questionable importance of the large dinner cloth, which a few years ago was considered the only correct linen for the dinner table. Today it is frequently replaced with placemats or runners, which formerly were considered correct only for breakfast and lunch.

The modern homemaker has justifiably discarded many of the previously accepted customs. Modern trends of meal planning and service have introduced homemakers to fewer courses, fewer foods in one course, and better choice of foods requiring less preparation. Also, the abundance of labor-saving tools assisting the homemaker has theoretically eliminated the need for paid help.

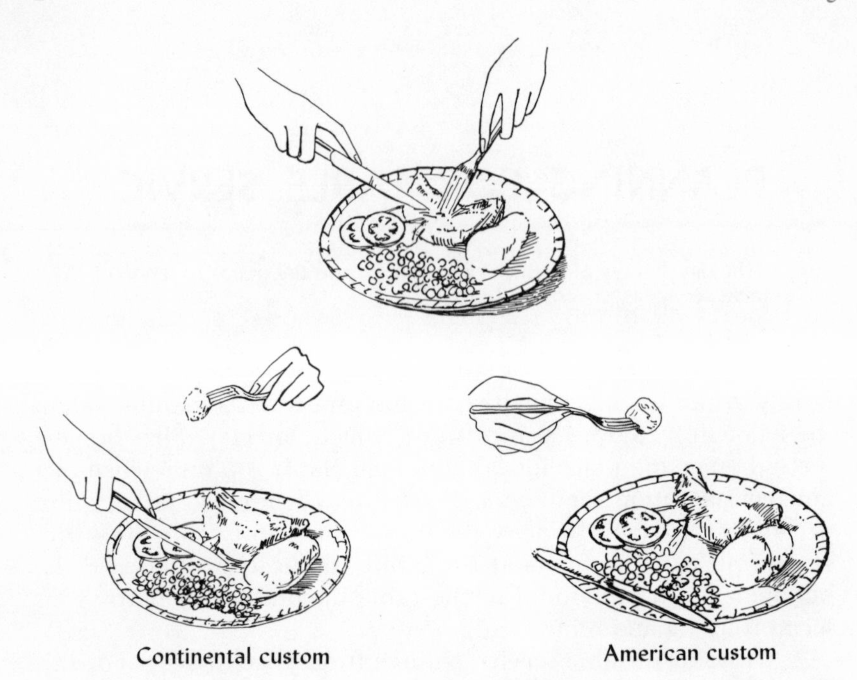

Continental custom American custom

However, it is important to keep in mind that though table service appears to be relatively simple, intelligent menu and service planning are still necessities. The ideal hostess without employed service will not attempt the formalities of table service observed by one with employed service, for service can become painfully difficult when the kitchen claims only one pair of hands. A hostess with good taste and intelligence plans to do only as much as she can do well and easily. A course omitted will never be noticed in the enjoyment of a dinner attractively and conveniently served by a hostess who is charming and at ease, who is able to mingle with her guests rather than merely to eavesdrop from the kitchen. For important functions, it may be worthwhile to engage additional help who will prepare basic foods or assist in kitchen duties in order to free the hostess for specialty tasks of preparing her choice foods, arranging flowers, or entertaining her guests.

The mere words "table service" and "table etiquette" seem to impregnate many with dread. It is important to realize the fact that good form is not adherence to an arbitrary set of rules. Service, as such, should never be in evidence, but rather, like well-oiled machinery, it should keep the meal going smoothly without anyone being especially conscious of it.

To be a successful hostess, every homemaker should know how to:

1. Prepare and serve simple foods in an appetizing manner.
2. Maintain and direct conversation.
3. Carry on table service with no disturbance or annoyance to those at the table.
4. Set a convenient and attractive table service for dining or buffet service.
5. Plan artistic arrangements of well-chosen table decorations.

Chapter 2

BEAUTIFUL TABLES

"The eye is the first to the feast . . ."

Wherever you live, however you entertain, whatever the climate, consider the pleasures experienced from eating meals which are planned and prepared to be appetizing and attractive as well as delicious and nutritious.

Entertaining has become increasingly easy, informal, and fun. The formal protocol of state dinners requiring white ties, elegant gowns, and lavish decorations has generally been replaced with more relaxed customs. Table appointments today are styled and priced to fit many budgets and the many settings in which meals are served. It is up to the hostess to create attractive settings, harmonizing food and mood, from the family meals to the late evening snacks to the more elaborate festive occasions enjoyed by every family. The most pleasing refreshments reach their maximum appeal when they are appetizingly prepared and attractively and easily served.

How is an appetizing meal created?

Whatever the occasion for table service, it is helpful to ask step by step questions, then check the setting after it is complete to note if at least the basic qualifications for an attractive meal have been observed or fulfilled.

Menu

Does the menu include foods which not only complement the flavors, but which also look appetizing in combination?

1. Are bland foods accented by foods with distinctive flavors?
2. Are soft foods complemented with crisp foods?
3. Are "whole" portions of food served with "diced" foods?
4. Are various interesting colors rather than a monotonous combination of similar colors included in the menu?

Sandwich swirls with cheese and ham filling complement milk punch.

Colorful appetizer tray variety. Each is small, well-seasoned. Chilled cranberry juice with lemon wheel garnish.

Dinnerware

Does the serving dish or tray make the food as attractive as possible?

1. *Design.* Is it unusual or interesting in shape or form? Is it functional and appropriate for the type and consistency of food served? (See pages 6 and 7.)
2. *Color.* Does it highlight the food and yet remain a background interest?
3. *Texture.* Does it complement, not compete with, the textures of the food served? Does it harmonize with the spirit of the occasion?

Table Linens

Do the linens present a beautiful and interesting background for the food and dinnerware?

1. Are the colors and textures appropriate?
2. Are the linens freshly laundered and carefully pressed?
3. Are the napkins neatly folded and accurately placed at each setting?
4. If a tablecloth or runners are used, do they hang evenly at the sides and ends of the table?
5. If placemats are used, does the shape harmonize with the shape of the table? Are they in scale with the food served?

Convenience and Comfort

Are the food and tableware conveniently placed for the diners?

1. Is there enough room between place settings? (See page 26.)
2. Is the flatware arranged in order of use?
3. Is the flatware placed approximately an inch from the edge of the table?
4. Are the place settings and chairs coordinated?
5. Is there enough total space allowed to provide a sufficient background for the food or accessory items?
6. Are the accessory items placed where they are easily accessible without interfering with serving or eating?
7. Has a place been provided for eating the meal with ease and comfort if buffet service is used?

Over-all Appearance

Is the finished table service *completely* attractive for the occasion?

1. Are the glasses and dishes sparkling clean?
2. Is the flatware freshly polished?
3. Is the centerpiece fresh and neatly arranged?
4. Is the centerpiece large enough so it does not look dwarfed, yet not so large that it dominates the table? Is it low enough to carry on a conversation with guests on the opposite side of the table?
5. Are style, texture, and color of dinnerware, flatware, glassware, and table napery harmonious?

Restraint in choice and number of dishes, as well as in the selection of linens and table decorations, is a keynote to success. The charm and beauty of food service are achieved through simplicity, not overdecoration.

Chapter 3

TABLE APPOINTMENTS

"Here is a hostess with taste and distinction . . ."

Your Table Expresses You

Of the hundreds of tables you normally set each year, you may not wish to, nor find it necessary to, create minor masterpieces each time. However, it is one activity, simple or elaborate, in which you can reflect your personality if you have the courage to openly express your sensitivity to design and texture, your feeling for color and balance, your awareness or "know how" of appropriate selections. Table settings provide a delightful opportunity to stimulate your imagination and exercise your creative talents.

In a home, the furniture, floor and wall coverings must team up well to make livable and inviting rooms. On the table, linens, flatware, dinnerware, and glassware need to be compatible to succeed in achieving harmoniously beautiful or handsome backgrounds for meals. If you wish to acquire the enviable reputation of "being a hostess with taste and distinction," first gain confidence in your knowledge of "what goes with what," then make your selections according to the mood you wish to create in the setting in which you are serving meals.

Variety and interest may be easily obtained today with even the slightest creative efforts because the range of textures and colors is so broad and interesting and available at any price. Your setting may be as formal or casual as you like it! The smoother and finer the textures and the more subtle the coloring and design, the more elegant is the setting. The heavier and rougher the texture and the more colorful the print or design, the more casual is the table service.

The setting may be as formal or as casual as the occasion dictates.

Table Linens

"Table linens" is a term referring to coverings used to complete table settings or protect table surfaces. It includes napkins and coverings ranging from the traditional large, linen-damask cloths to individual placemats or table runners. Of all materials, fabric and non-fabric, linen remains the first choice for most hostesses because of its natural crispness and low gloss. The treasured white or ivory linen-damask, the "Aristocrat of Table Linens," formerly a must for a well-set table, is rarely used today except in formal contemporary or traditional settings when it provides a background for beautiful and fine table accessories. In its place lovely colors of damask or plainly woven linen and other textured fabrics have appeared. These fabrics meet the request for good-looking linens which harmonize with moderately priced table appointments, as well as meet the demand for fabrics which are less time consuming in laundry care. This change reflects trends to more informal table service and settings in which variety of color and texture is desirable.

Luncheon cloths, placemats, bridge sets, and napkins are often made of plainly woven fabrics with rough and interesting textures. They are available in a variety of fibers—linen, cotton, synthetic fibers, or blends. Use of placemats should be encouraged as they lend a spirit of informality and also save time consumed in laundering large cloths.

To receive maximum esthetic and economic satisfaction from any linens purchased, it is advantageous to know the fiber content as well as the cost, expected performance, and care. Labels attached to the linens will provide this information for you.

Cloths and mats emphasizing utilitarian value have also been designed and appreciated for specific functions. The plastic or other synthetic coverings make no special claim to beauty, but they are quickly and easily cleaned, and are basically an economic saving for a family with children. Cork, bamboo, straw, and paper have also become favorites because of their easy care as well as interesting rustic textures. Harmonizing paper or fabric napkins may be used with any of these coverings.

The choice of pattern and color of table linens greatly influences the character of the table service. Linens in fine checks or large plaids cast a carefree spell on the setting. Floral or fruit designs, especially in vivid colors, also produce a happy and bright atmosphere. Provincial and peasant stripes tend to be entertaining,

Harmonious textures and patterns enhance the total setting.

Table linens influence the mood of the setting.

while subdued and subtle designs tend to be conservative and quieting. It is up to you to pick a pattern that suits the occasion and harmonizes with your table appointments. All other surfaces must be subordinated to that main interest. You may use plain linens with undecorated appointments and plain linens with patterned appointments very effectively. However, patterned linens with patterned appointments will only create a blur, losing the beauty of both background and foreground in a sea of design. Only one pattern may be the dominant point of interest.

The rainbow of colors from which to make your selection is exciting. Try to harmonize the colors found in linens with your china either through repetition or through the blending of colors, or by accenting the color of dinnerware with a contrasting hue. Dainty pastels are feminine and pretty; dark colors are masculine and rustic; cool colors are refreshing and distinctive; warm tones are cheerful and inviting; neutrals are subtle and dignified. Table appointments can be complemented and food can be made more appetizing when sparked with colorful linens!

The size and shape of table coverings you select are determined by the size and shape of your dining table, dining counter, or whatever area you design for eating purposes. Buy your coverings to fit and look well in a particular space. To achieve harmony between table covering and table, the covering itself, or the designs woven or printed into the coverings, need to repeat the shape of the table which is used. For example, a plaid tablecloth is more beautiful on a square or rectangular table than on a round table.

Buy a tablecloth suitable for the normal length of your table or for one extended length which you most frequently use. The desirable drop of a tablecloth is eight to twelve inches from the table's edge. Too short a tablecloth is unattractive; too long a cloth will interfere with the comfort of the guests. The only tablecloth which may touch the floor is a banquet cloth.

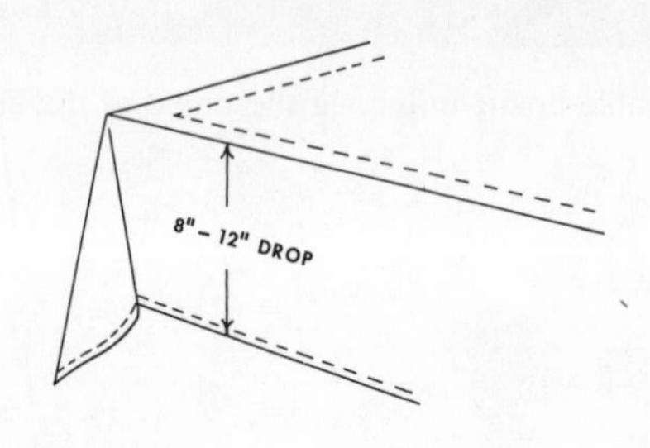

Placemats and runners are designed in varying sizes. An adequate background will enhance both meal and setting; whereas, one which is too small or too large will detract from the beauty of the setting. Select whatever size is in scale with the table setting you are using. For example, a dessert setting does not require as large a mat as one needed for a dinner setting.

Napkins

Though napkins were designed for very functional purposes, they may also lend a spot of interest to the table. Formal tablecloths with napkins to match are sold as a unit. However, for the less formal cloth, napkins are purchased separately to offer a greater variety of combinations. Napkins of contrasting colors, gayly woven, printed, or plain in color could readily become exciting accents for table settings. Today paper napkins are also available in a wide range of colors, sizes, and textures. Their color selection should be considered as carefully as the fabric napkin since they, too, need to fit into the scheme of the general setting.

The most desirable characteristics of all napkins are that they be absorbent and soft in texture. Smooth, sleek surfaces are not only non-functional but are also difficult to keep in place; rough, harsh surfaces are not pleasing to the touch.

Napkins are designed in various sizes to correspond with the needs of many types of entertaining. The usual sizes are:

Dinner napkins:	18, 20, 22, 24 inches square
Luncheon and breakfast napkins:	17 inches square
Tea napkins:	12 inches square
"Lapkins":	12 x 18 inches

Silence Cloth or Table Pad

One of the delightful features of gracious dining as opposed to casual eating is the silence with which tableware and serving dishes are handled at the table. The silence cloth or table pad used under the table covering is partly responsible for this pleasure. As the name implies, sounds created by contacts made between the hard surfaces of dinnerware, glassware, or silverware and the table are muffled. Of equal importance is the protection they provide for the surface of the table against moisture and heat.

Silence cloths are made from a variety of fabrics. Felt and quilted fabrics have been satisfactorily used, whereas, bonded fabrics with foam backing are questionable since tableware will not stand firmly on too spongy a fabric. These cloths are not cut to fit the size of the table, but rather they are cut large enough to allow a drop at the sides and ends of the table, in order to give a smooth, graceful drape to the tablecloth.

For absolute protection against heat and moisture, folding pads may be custom made to fit the shape and size of the table. Extra pads may be ordered for the leaves used in extending the table. They are constructed of a rigid material covered with felt on one side and with a heat and moisture-resistant material on the opposite side.

It is advisable to use pads or silence cloths under placemats and table runners. They help to keep the smaller coverings in place on the hard finished surfaces, as well as contribute to the silence of a well set table. The silence pad or cloth used with tablecloths or other types of table coverings should never be conspicuous.

Tableware Trousseau

Tableware and table linens serve as tools for gracious entertaining. As you build your collection of tableware (dinnerware, flatware, and glassware), it is important that you consider not only the beauty and quality of individual items, but also recognize each as a basic part of one picture.

How is it possible to arrive at a decision for a selection of tableware when faced with such a multitude of choices in each area?

First of all, ask yourself what type of entertaining you will do. Will it be mainly formal dinners, informal buffet suppers or family meals, bridge luncheons or patio meals? Then attempt to establish the general characteristics associated with the mood of your most enjoyed table service. Does your taste lie in the highly decorative or ornate design, or do you prefer intermediate patterns with little design, or the plain patterns with no decorative design? Do you favor the finer textures of formal settings or the coarse texture of the informal?

A true analysis also entails recognizing the differences and similarities of character reflected by the existing textures of tableware. Flatware ranges from gleaming silver to the soft glow of stainless steel, to the bright finish of Dirilyte. Beautiful glassware is reflected in the brilliancy of crystal, as well as in the clearness of heavy glass. The scope of dinnerware extends from the lovely translucency of china to the rustic appearance of earthenware to the practicality of the melamines. By recognizing characteristic textures of each, your decisions in making choices will be simplified. An attractive table setting relates texture and structural design of tableware and allows freedom in blending ideas and intermingling patterns. By concentrating on coordinating moods, harmonizing textures, and blending colors, you will find your efforts interesting and rewarding when mixing new with old, contemporary with traditional.

What general characteristics of tableware assure most satisfactory use?

Dinnerware:

1. Are the shapes practical?
2. Are the dishes easy to handle?
3. Are the dishes comfortable to handle?
4. Do dishes have a rolled edge, thickened or rounded, to give a better resistance to chipping?
5. Do cup and pitcher handles offer a firm grip?
6. Is the well of the plate sufficiently deep to hold the food?
7. Are the plates and platters designed with a shallow foot to provide an easy grasp and contribute to heat deflection from the table surface?

Flatware:

1. Are the tines of the forks, bowls of the spoons, blades of the knives all in good proportion to the handles?
2. Are the edges of the bowls of the spoons and tines of the forks smooth?
3. Does the structural design of each piece feel comfortable when held?
4. Does each feel well balanced in your hand?
5. Are the decorative lines graceful?

Glassware

1. Are the edges smooth—free of chips or cracks?
2. Does the glassware feel balanced when handled?

3. Is the glassware free of streaks and bubbles, except in fine blown glass? (Streaks are not to be confused with rings which are sometimes evident in glass. They are caused by the variation of density of glass, designed for a specific purpose. Example: Rim of a wine glass will be thinner than the base.)
4. Are the details of the design clear and distinct?

After having decided on your choice of individual designs, but before making your final decision, view one or two total place settings to visualize how individual choices will appear in a finished setting and how the total setting will appear in repetition. It is important that the combination of all designs results in *one* beautiful, attractive picture, and that repeated settings magnify their beauty rather than become monotonous in overuse.

Later, when planning meals and table service, a number of other factors may influence specific choices of appointments for a particular occasion. A natural source of inspiration is the menu itself. For example, a meal consisting of barbecued chicken with hot biscuits and tossed, green salad suggests casual sociability—perhaps a picnic or patio supper. It is natural that such a meal could be served on pottery with stainless steel flatware, tumblers or mugs, on a checkered tablecloth with paper napkins. Another deciding factor may be the assortment and variety of table linens available. Since linens serve as the background interest which unify textures, colors, and the mood of tableware, they definitely play a role in dictating the choice of desirable tableware. The "special occasion" meal often planned around a central theme also determines appointments used.

Centerpiece—Just the Right Touch!

That colorful and interesting centerpiece may not wend its way to each of your table settings, but without a question it is that decorative touch added to table service which gives personality to your table. It is often referred to as the "final finishing touch." In reality, it may play an important part in providing the "introductory touch" as well as an interesting conversation at your table. A beautiful flower floating in crystal clear water, the unusual container from a far distant trip, the ingenious combination of textures and colors of fruit, the creative use of interesting shapes of cacti roots, the clever arrangement of potted plants, the rich green tone of shiny lemon leaves in a straw basket, the brilliance of glassware emphasized with glimmering candlelight—each will arouse someone's curiosity sufficiently to invite conversation. Just the right centerpiece will highlight table appointments as well as create a festive atmosphere in the dining area.

The centerpiece, simple or elaborate, must be in scale with the serving table and so placed that it will not interfere with conversation or comfort. If too large, it is best placed at the end of the table or perhaps on a nearby side table. If it is too small, it will automatically lose its charm, and the efforts expended in arrangement will go unrewarded.

Chapter 4

SETTING THE TABLE

"There's delight in knowing how."

Hospitality and sociability between family and friends have always been closely associated with the pleasures of eating. How or why did practices in table setting evolve? Rules of table setting, like other patterns of etiquette, have gradually developed as tried practices have proved to be desirable. The placement of flatware, for example, contributes to the ease and gracefulness in eating a meal because an orderly arrangement of knives, forks, or spoons is easier to handle than if they are arranged in a haphazard fashion. By following generally accepted patterns, table setting becomes a natural ritual, simply and easily done for any meal at anyone's home.

The table may be set as formally or as casually as you like it but correct and efficient table settings are always important. The basic recipe for this understanding is in knowing the traditional rules. Whether you use damask cloths or straw mats, china or plastic, sterling silver or stainless steel, a general understanding of correct settings is the key blender for the tastefully set table. Within their framework, you may be as creative as the situation allows. Use them as a guide—do not be hampered by them.

Setting a table is a joy if you keep a few simple suggestions in mind.

Much of a table's attractiveness will depend upon the mathematical precision with which each piece is laid. In setting the table, place the largest plates to be used for the meal first in order to space the settings uniformly, to establish the distance between them, and to note the exact position of the flatware. Place settings should be equidistant from the ends of the table. If an even number is set, the settings should be exactly opposite each other. To keep the settings harmonious, all the lines of the setting (straight-lined designs in the tableware as well as in the linens) should be parallel or perpendicular to the table. (See page 79.)

Flatware is placed in correct sequence with regard to its use, from the outside of the setting toward the center. Place the pieces close together without crowding. This gives a setting the appearance of a complete unit. The distance at which the flatware is placed from the edge of the table will vary from three-fourths inch to one inch, depending upon the size and shape of the table. Today's custom requires setting only the pieces that will actually be used. To avoid confusion and an "overdone" appearance, no more than three pieces are usually placed at each side. Exceptions may occur if the setting is very wide, or if the fourth piece is small. With the informal table service, the extra flatware may be placed by the hostess as she serves courses at the table.

Table Service: One Place Setting

A place setting is a complete service for one person. Each place setting consists of five or six pieces of dinnerware and flatware. In addition, it includes one glass for each type of beverage served plus one sherbet glass.

DINNERWARE: In the five-piece place setting the soup bowl is omitted.

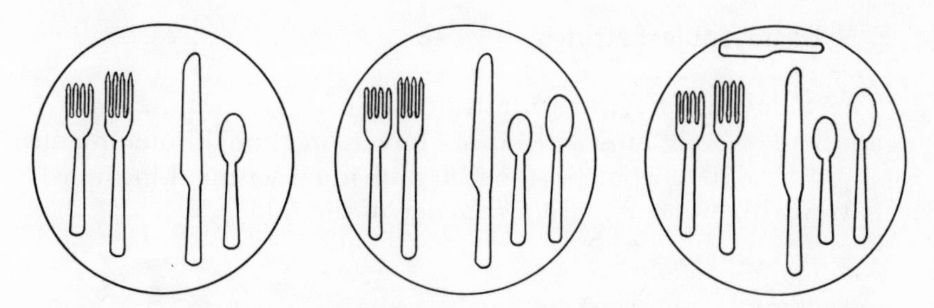

FLATWARE: In the five-piece place setting the cream soup spoon or a second teaspoon is interchangeable.

STEMWARE: Glassware with foot and stem.

TUMBLERS: Glassware with or without foot but without stem.

Basic Table Settings

The following diagrams illustrate table settings which may be adapted to suit most breakfast, luncheon, and dinner menus:

Allow 20 to 24 inches for each individual setting. Line up your flatware about *one inch* from the edge of the table.

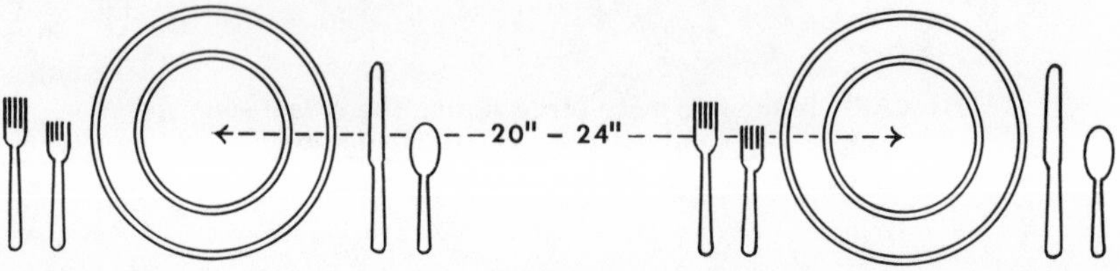

20" – 24"

Spacing individual settings.

Knives and *spoons* are placed on the right, the sharp edge of the knife toward the inside, the bowls of the spoons up. The butter spreader, if used, is placed across the top of the butter plate slightly above the center, parallel to the edge of the table with the spreading edge toward the inside and the handle to the right.

Forks are placed at the left with the tines up. When the salad fork is placed to the left of the dinner fork, the salad is served as the first course or part of the main course. When the salad fork is placed next to the dinner plate, the salad is served after the main course, or the fork will serve as the dessert fork.

The *water glass* is placed at the right about one-half inch from the tip of the knife. Whether it is placed above or at the right of the tip will depend upon the depth or width of the setting. The shape of the placemats—round, square, or oblong—may affect the placing. The smaller juice glass is placed between the water glass and the plate, slightly lower than the water glass.

The *bread-and-butter plate* is placed at the left above the fork. It is sometimes shifted to the right or left if a salad is served with the dinner. The bread-and-butter plate is omitted from the formal dinner setting.

A *salad* or *dessert fork* or *dessert spoon*, is placed at the right of the plate if it is the only piece of flatware on the table.

BEGINNING OF MEAL

DESSERT

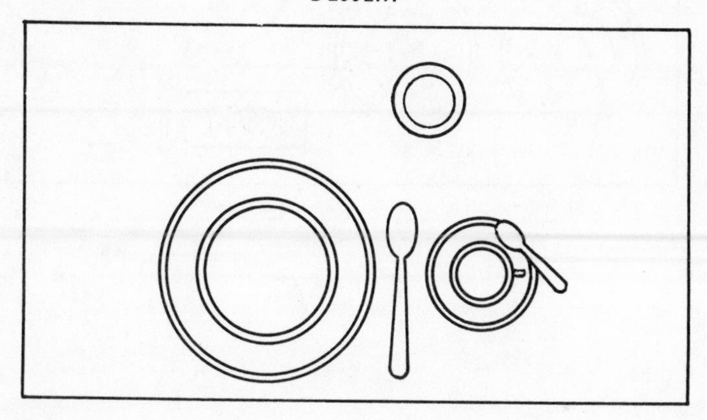

Variety in Food Service

Trays

Set a buffet tray or TV table tray as an individual place setting. If space is limited, omit the butter plate. Spread rolls in advance and serve from a bread plate or basket.

Buffet

For a buffet or tea, table appointments look best when groups of appointments are placed parallel to each other. Never place pieces of flatware on top of one another. Flatware may be alternated (see page 29) or may be in separate groups of knives, forks, spoons.

Tea

For informal service, the tea or coffee spoon may be placed with the cup on the saucer before it is served.

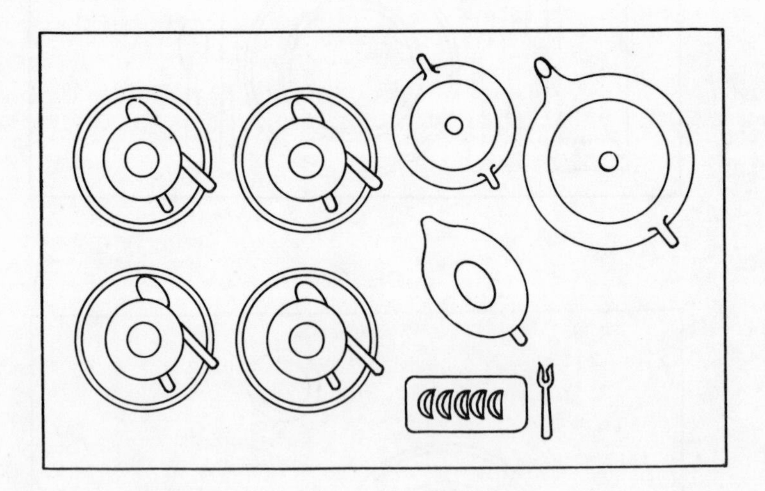

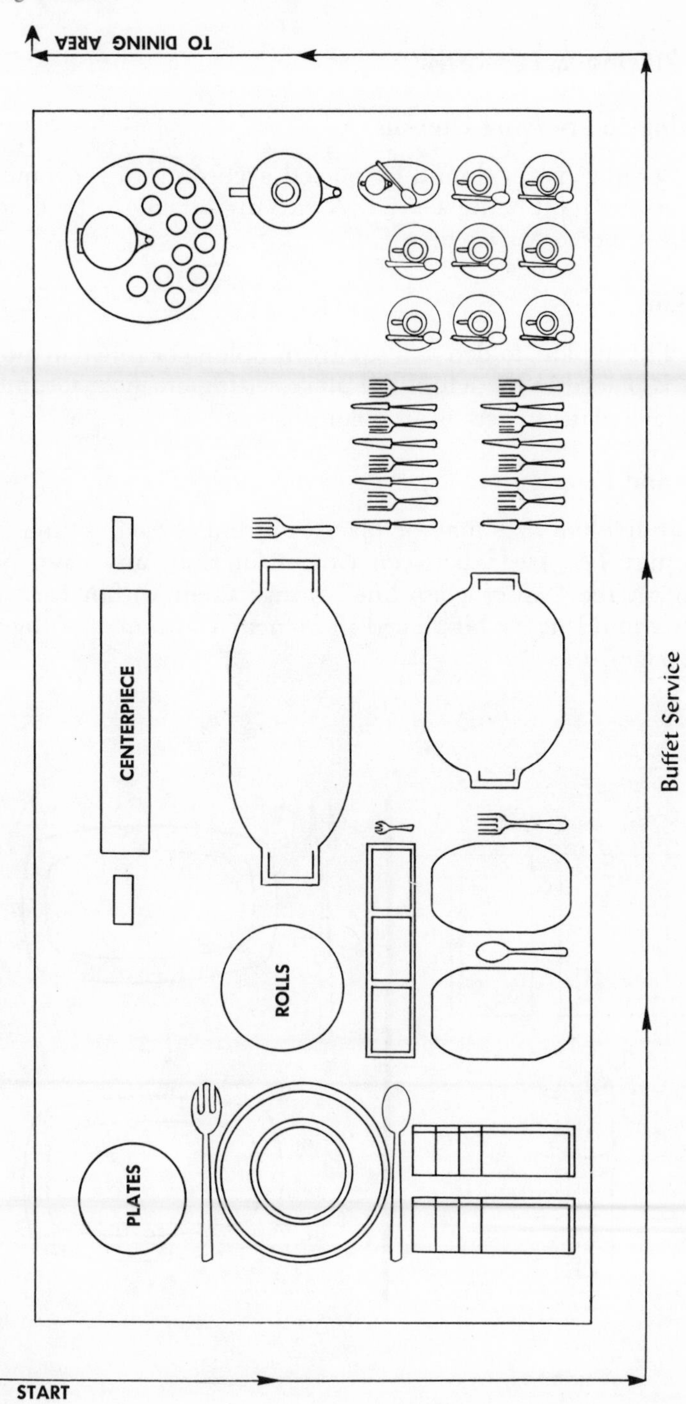

Buffet Service

Placing Accessories

Carving and Serving Utensils

Serving pieces should be placed according to convenience—next to the food being served. A carving set might be placed in either of the ways shown.

Napkins

The napkin, folded as a square or oblong or rolled in a napkin ring, is placed to the left of the place setting or, more formally, on the place plate, folded as an oblong.

Salts and Peppers

Individual sizes may be placed in front of each setting, or one pair may be placed between two settings. In any case, placing them on the "water glass line" brings them within easy reach. They should never be placed in or near the center of the table. (See page 79.)

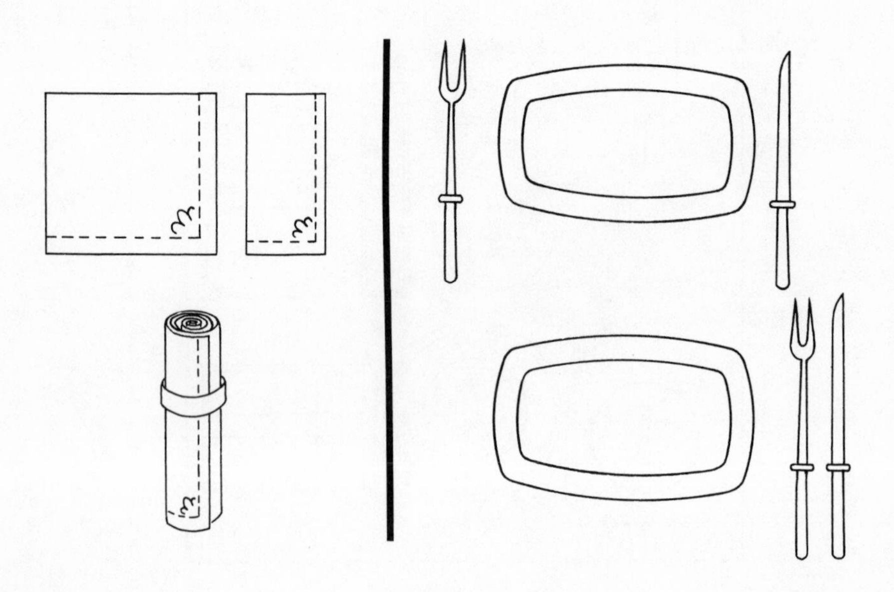

Placing the Jelly, Bread and Butter, Pickles, etc.

These foods should be so placed that they are within easy reach. Any accompanying flatware should be placed on the table at the side of the bowl with the handle parallel to the table's edge pointing toward the person responsible for passing it. These foods are placed on the table just before the meal is announced. Try to arrange all the extras conveniently and harmoniously, yet avoid having them merge into the center.

Placing the Chairs

When the table has been set, place the chairs so the line of the hanging cloth will not be broken. If placemats are used, observe the same distance from the table. This enables the guests to seat themselves with little or no moving of the chairs.

Confidently knowing that your table is correctly set adds to your poise as a hostess. It is simple to enjoy this assurance if you become well acquainted with the suggested practices of table settings which have proved to be attractive and convenient for many hostesses in the past. The aims of achieving correct table service should include knowledge of factors contributing to (1) ease of serving food; (2) convenience of flatware arrangement for eating purposes; (3) the achievement of balance and beauty of the table as a whole.

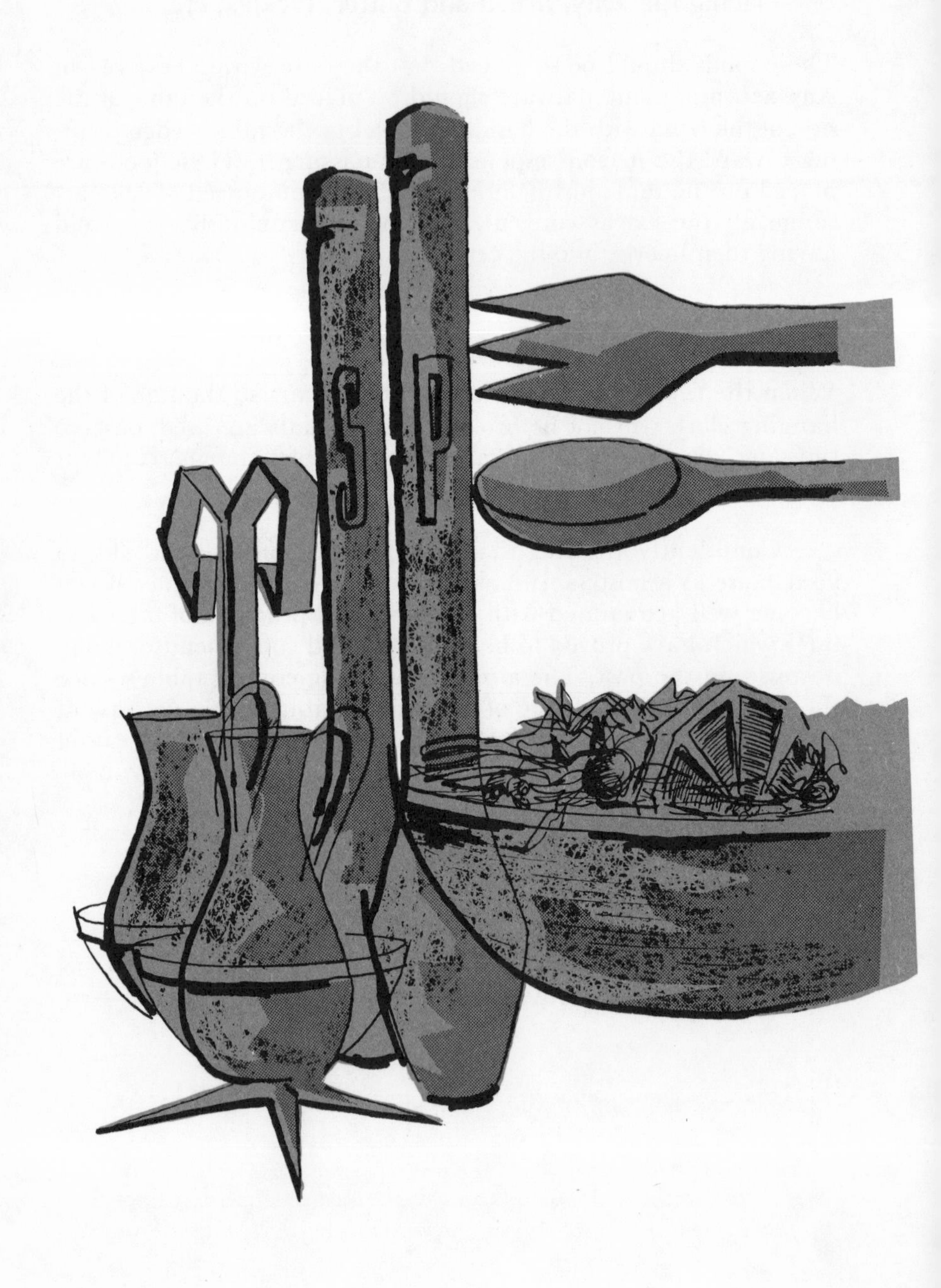
S
P

Chapter 5

GARNISHING OF FOOD

"Used to reveal, not to conceal the food."

Adherence to the laws of art and design is as necessary in making a dish attractive as in setting a table. So plebian a dish as a gruel can assume a festive air if it is but served "piping hot" in a blue or yellow bowl, with, as the late George Rector, a famous restaurateur and author, says, "the final gesture of a dash of paprika in the very center of a golden pool of melted butter."

Reasons for Garnishing Food

1. To make the dish more attractive.
   Though it is true that well-cooked food served in attractive dishes on a carefully laid, immaculate table needs little decoration, a touch of garnish will not only add a festive air to the meal but will also tempt the feeble appetite.
2. To add to the food value.
   Crackers or whipped cream served with soups and bouillon add energy-producing food to the basic serving.
3. To add bulk to a single dish or the meal.
   Celery tops, watercress, or vegetables are frequently served with meats. The contrast of flavors is pleasant, and the combination of foods increases the palatability of protein foods.

Characteristics of the Garnish

1. It should be edible and simple.
2. It should not look as though much time had been spent in its preparation. An exception might be made for the un-

Bun burgers with scrambled eggs and
Canadian bacon — the delight of all ages — are highlighted
with radish roses.

usual occasion when a theme is carried out as at a children's party.

3. It should be used sparingly. Garnish should reveal, not conceal the food. A dash of paprika or nutmeg is attractive, too much is offensive. A sprig of parsley should not become a bouquet. If a sauce is used, it is best not to saturate the food with the liquid.
4. It should be neatly placed. When using leaves, do not let the stems show. Never allow paprika to sprinkle on the edge of the plate or dish.
5. It should not interfere with the service. No part of the garnish should extend beyond the rim of the dinnerware. (See pages 6, 7 and 34.)

The Necessity of Garnishes and Accompaniments for Courses and Dishes

Tradition and custom have dictated certain garnishes or accompaniments for many of our foods. However, the hostess should not feel obligated to follow these traditions consistently. For example, the customary serving of applesauce with pork may suggest an opportunity for experimentation and originality. The combination of apples and pork is an excellent one from the standpoint of flavor. Added zest may be given in the preparation, and serving, if the apple appears as fried apple rings, apple pickles, spiced apples, or cinnamon apples. Also, apples may be combined with other foods as in apple dressing and scalloped apples and sweet potatoes. In the case of soup, not all varieties need to be garnished with paprika or chopped parsley; instead, think of the possibility of bread in various forms, diced vegetables, grated cheese, chopped peppers, fried onions, whipped cream, the Italian pastes, wafers, chopped hard-cooked eggs, asparagus tips, or puffed cereals.

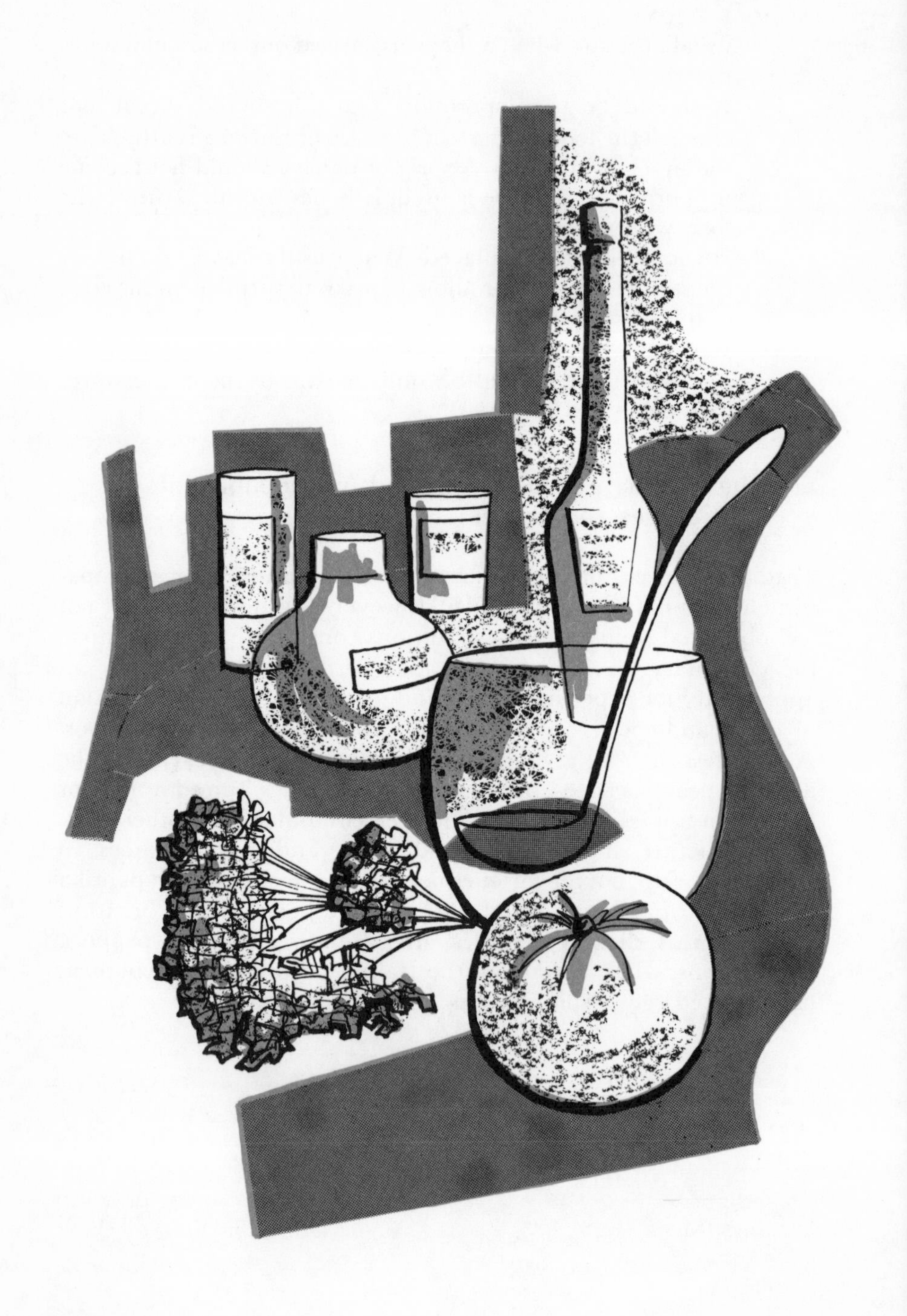

Chapter 6

SALAD SERVICE

"America's greatest contribution to the culinary art."

The salad is probably our most versatile of dishes. It may be served as the main course, as a separate course, preceding or following the main course, as an accompaniment to the main course, or as the dessert, depending upon the kind of meal. As such, it has many additional advantages, especially from the standpoint of family service.

1. It adds to the palatability of other foods served at that time.
2. It may reduce the number of vegetables prepared for the meat course.
3. If wisely chosen, it lessens last-minute preparations.
4. It adds attractiveness to the table, as it is usually on when the meal is announced.
5. It may shorten the time required for serving if placed before the meal is announced.

If the dinner is to be more elaborate from the standpoint of service and number of courses, the salad may appear as a separate course following the main course. In some sections of the country, it is served as a first course.

The Choice of Flatware

The choice of flatware used with the salad depends on the type of salad served, type of meal served, as well as the formality of the meal. A special salad knife and fork, the dinner fork alone, or a salad fork alone may be used. Salad forks are placed according to their sequence of use. If the salad precedes the main course or accompanies the meal, the fork is placed to the left of the dinner fork.

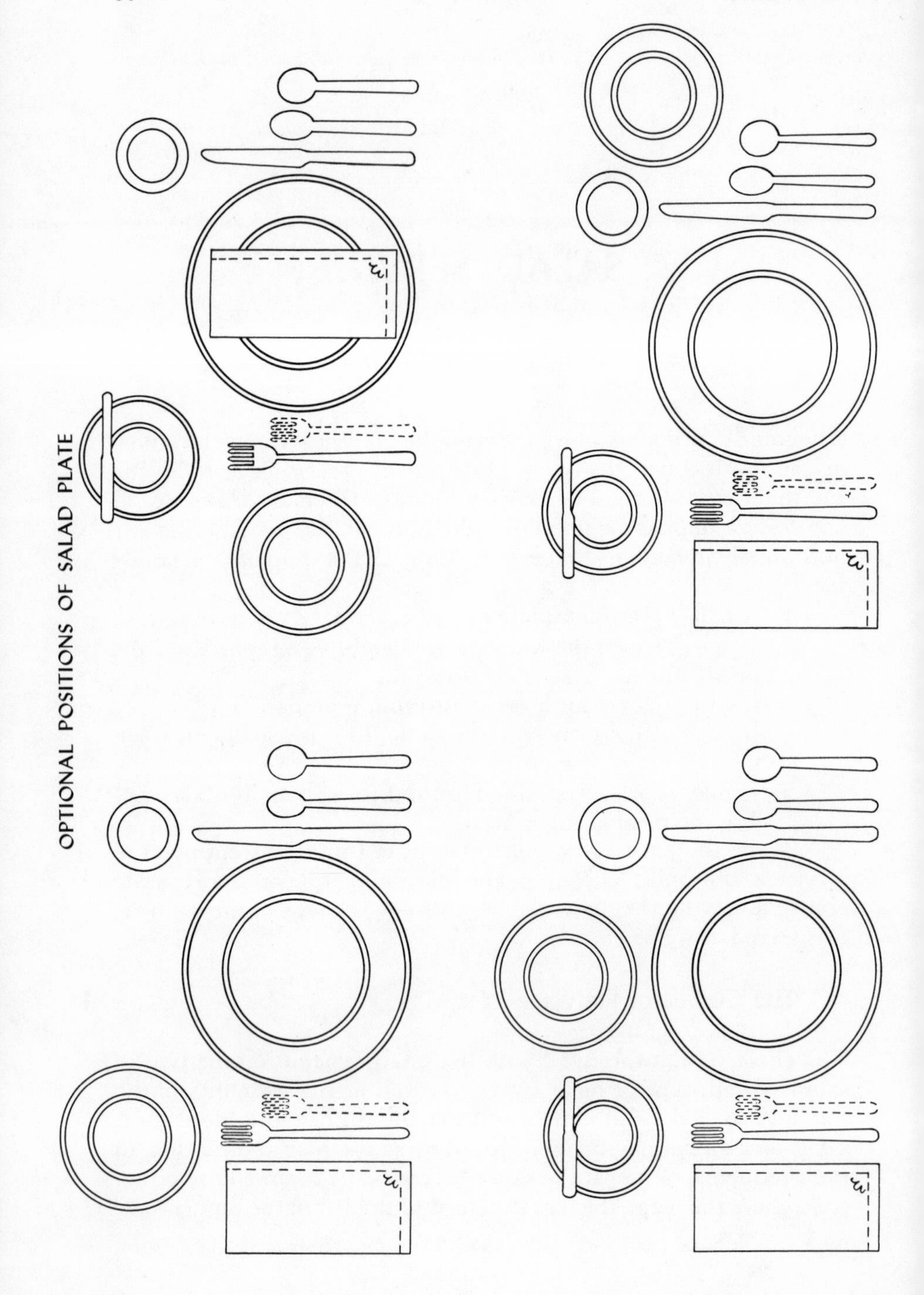
OPTIONAL POSITIONS OF SALAD PLATE

If the salad follows the meat course, the fork is placed between the dinner fork and the dinner plate.

For a less formal meal, when the salad is served with the meat course, the salad fork may be omitted. The salad fork may also be omitted if space between the settings is limited.

1. It avoids confusion, especially if that fork is planned for the dessert. (It would be better to place that fork later when the dessert is served.)
2. It lessens the number of soiled pieces of flatware.
3. It avoids exchanging one fork for the other, which frequently becomes embarrassing.
4. It conserves amount of space needed for each setting.

Placing the Salad Plate

The position of the salad plate is probably the most discussed and disputed question of table setting. A perusal of books on the subject leads to the conclusion that writers do not agree. As with other questions regarding table service, the question can best be answered by applying the basic principles of design and using judgment in thinking through the situation.

In determining the best position one must take into account factors such as size of table, shape of table (round or square), equipment available, service available, etc. Any one of four positions may be equally correct:

1. To the left and above the fork providing the bread-and-butter plate is omitted.
2. At the left slightly below the bread-and-butter plate or in line with the center of the dinner plate.
3. Above the dinner plate and to the right of the bread-and-butter plate. (The bread-and-butter plate may be shifted slightly more to the left.)
4. At the right and slightly below the water glass or in line with the center of the dinner plate.

Placing the salad on the left (1 or 2) is preferred because it affords excellent leverage in cutting, which is essential to the comfortable eating of most salads. This location also facilitates the removing of the setting at the end of the dinner course since both may be cleared from one side. On the right, the salad may inter-

Salad bowl pièce de résistance for the buffet or family dinner table.

fere with the ease in refilling water glasses, as well as with the serving of a beverage.

The present practice of using a plate of dessert size for the dinner salad, leaving room for butter and bread, is commendable. It lessens the number of dishes, avoids a crowded appearance, and makes it easier to clear the table at the end of the dinner course.

Serving Salads

A delightful practice, if the hostess prefers, is to serve the salad at the table. This may be done in three ways:

1. Individual nests of lettuce may be filled with the salad mixture, garnished appropriately, and placed on a large platter or chop plate. This service is convenient and attractive for the plate dinner or luncheon.
2. A bowl may be lined with crisp salad greens, and the mixed and seasoned ingredients spooned into the center.
3. The salad materials may be tossed together lightly at the table just before serving.

For the convenience of the hostess, place the salad plate or bowl directly in front of the hostess, with the individual plates to the right or left or directly in front of the salad bowl. A large spoon and fork or two large spoons may be placed on each side of the setting.

Salad Accompaniments

An accompaniment or "pusher" is essential for ease and comfort in eating some types of salads, especially when served as a separate course. These are probably more appreciated as aids if the fork is the only utensil provided. Crackers of all varieties, bread sticks, cheese straws, cheese biscuits, finger rolls, wafers, sandwiches, and toast are appropriate.

Chapter 7

CARVING SKILLS AND SERVING KNOWHOW

"May I serve you?"

The friendly atmosphere created through the active participation of the host and hostess in serving food to guests readily contributes to congenial fellowship at mealtime. Since all the food for the course is on the table, or on adjacent tables within easy reach of the host and hostess, it provides the opportunity for a meal to be served with relatively little effort.

Carving should be encouraged at the family table as well as for guest meals. It can set the stage for a relaxed time of fellowship and an exchange of family interests. In addition, it is an ideal time for the host to develop the enviable skill of artful carving and graceful serving to dinner guests.

Satisfactory Carving Depends upon Several Factors

1. A knowledge of the anatomy of the meat or poultry which is to be carved with regard to bones, joints, structure, and direction of muscle fiber.
2. Good tools with which to work.
   A sharp, long-bladed knife, a two-tined fork usually with a guard, and a steel constitute a basic or standard carving set. Other carving tools will be noted in the carving directions for specific meats and poultry which follow.
3. Availability of a large platter, sizable enough to accommodate the garnish and the necessary servings. Unless the platter is of such a size, an extra plate or small platter should be provided for additional servings of meat.
4. Properly cooked meat or poultry — neither overdone nor underdone. (See pages 49 and 54.)

Carving and Serving—Tips for Hostess and Host

1. It may be desirable for the host to visit the kitchen for special instructions before the meal is served.
2. The roasting schedule should be planned so that meat or poultry "can rest" 15 to 30 minutes in the roast-pan after it is done. This firms the meat, the juices will be absorbed, the meat will be easier to carve, and time will be allowed for last minute tasks.
3. Skewers, toothpicks, cord or strings used in tying and trussing meat and poultry should be removed in the kitchen.
4. Frills or cuffs may be placed over drumstick ends or a crown roast. (See pages 49 and 54.) Paper napkins, neatly folded and held in place securely under the platter's edge, are helpful also to the carver.
5. Platter and plates should be prewarmed since servings cool quickly.
6. The platter is usually placed above the plates in front of the host. Occasionally, it may be more convenient for carving to place the platter directly in front of the host with the plates at the left or the right. (See page 79.) In whatever location, the platter is placed so near the dinner plates that the latter need not be lifted in serving.
7. The carver may sit or stand to his task. Most skilled carvers prefer to stand. In any case, he should be given plenty of room.
8. The carving is done from right to left so that the carved portions of meat or poultry are on the right side of the platter, thereby facilitating ease in serving. (See pages 49 and 50.) Rare and well-done, fat and lean portions are noted by the carver to accommodate preferences. The location and expert removal of choice morsels may be important to satisfy some requests.
9. Enough meat is carved before serving to adequately serve everyone. An exception to this might be when meat is heavily planked with vegetables and it becomes necessary to displace some of the vegetables to an extra plate. This may be done before beginning to carve, as well as during the carving process.
10. Most meats are carved across the grain of the cut. This cuts the muscle fibers, thus avoiding a stringy texture. Steaks are cut with the grain as are some parts of poultry.

11. Serve fairly small portions to prevent the waste of too large a serving, or to grant guests the opportunity to be served second servings of food they desire.
12. Using one or two serving spoons eases the transfer of serving food from the platter to the individual plates.
13. Ordinarily, the meat is placed first and at the top of the plate. This puts it in position for better cutting leverage, especially if knife and fork are both needed for cutting.
14. Do not overcrowd the plate, nor place food too near the edge, nor too close together. Space must be allowed for the knife and fork to rest. Food looks much more appetizing when a small amount of background space surrounds it.
15. Usually a bit of the garnish is served, thus carrying the original attractiveness of the platter to each service. This necessitates individual garnishes to be scaled to the size of dinner plates rather than to the size of the platter.
16. It is best to have the gravy served by the person at the right of the host. Another custom is to pass the gravy around the table, allowing each guest to serve himself according to his wishes.
17. The host states distinctly for whom the plate is intended. The first plate is served to the hostess or to the guest of honor. If the dinner party is small in number, the second is served to the guest at the right of the hostess, continuing on the right side of the table up to the host. The service then begins to the left of the hostess.
18. When the host has finished carving and serving, the carving tools and serving tools may be placed on the platter. The platter and auxiliary serving dishes may then be removed to a service cart or to a warming oven. Carving and serving tools are removed lest they be damaged by the heat. If quickly washed and wiped they will be ready to be returned to the table for second servings use. The host should delay preparing second servings since they cool quickly.
19. The hostess is first asked to be re-served. She is obliged to take a second serving of some food in order that guests feel free to accept more food, if they so desire.

BEEF BLADE POT ROAST

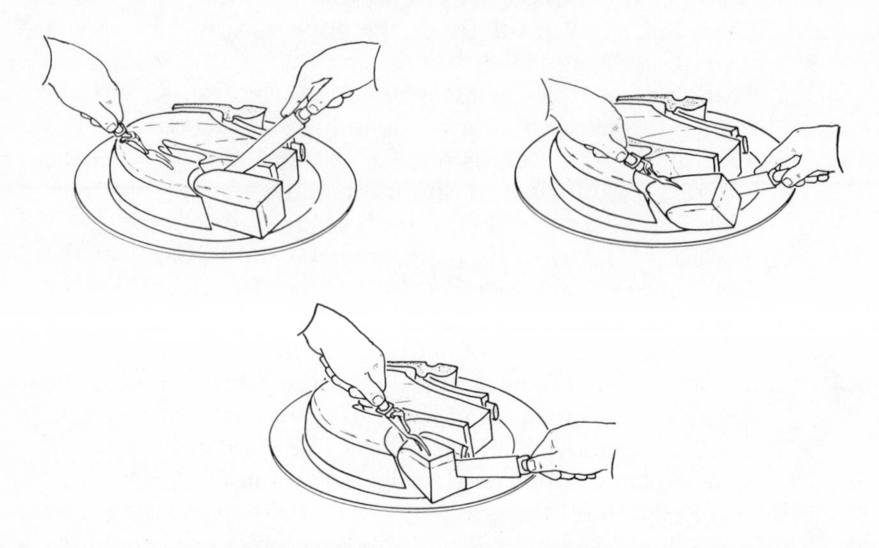

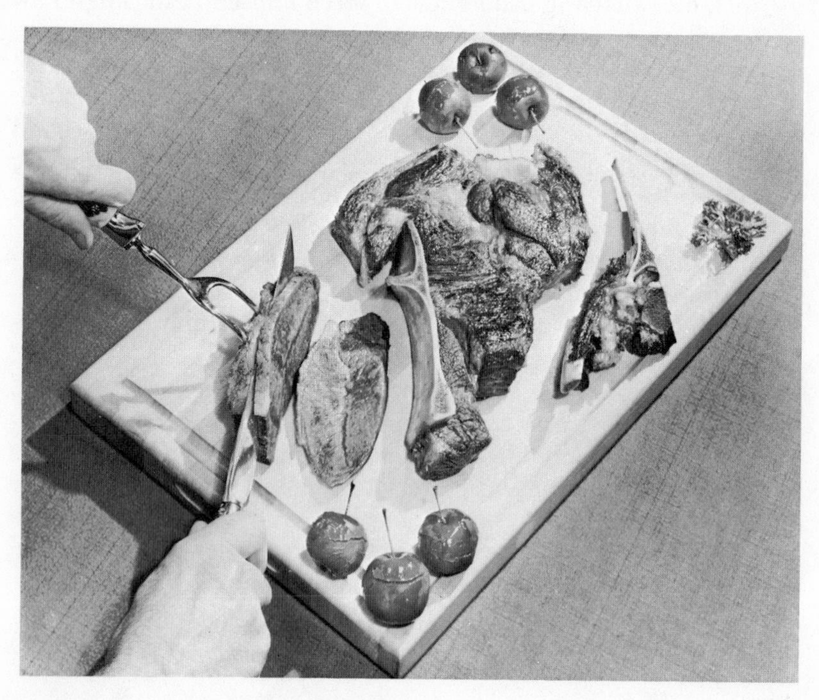

Correct carving assures uniform servings.

SHANK HALF OF HAM

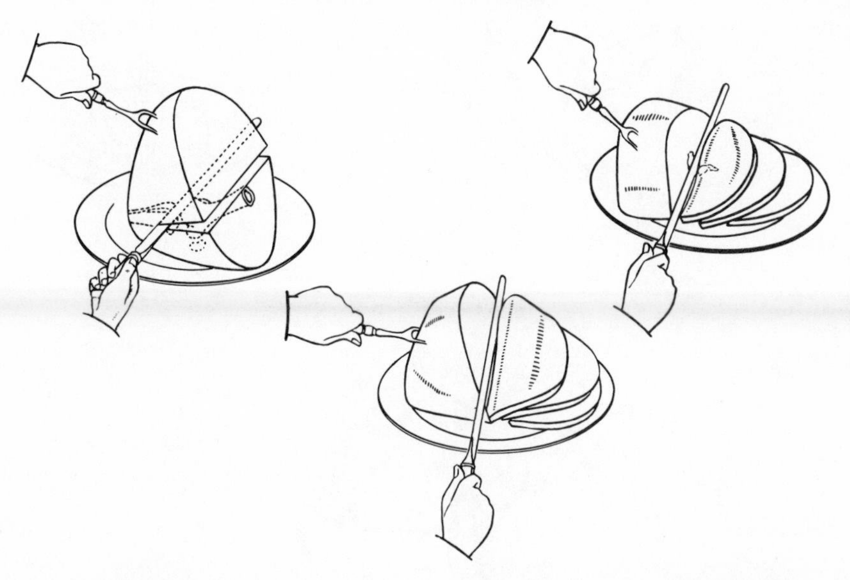

First cut is made close to the bone.

BUTT HALF OF HAM

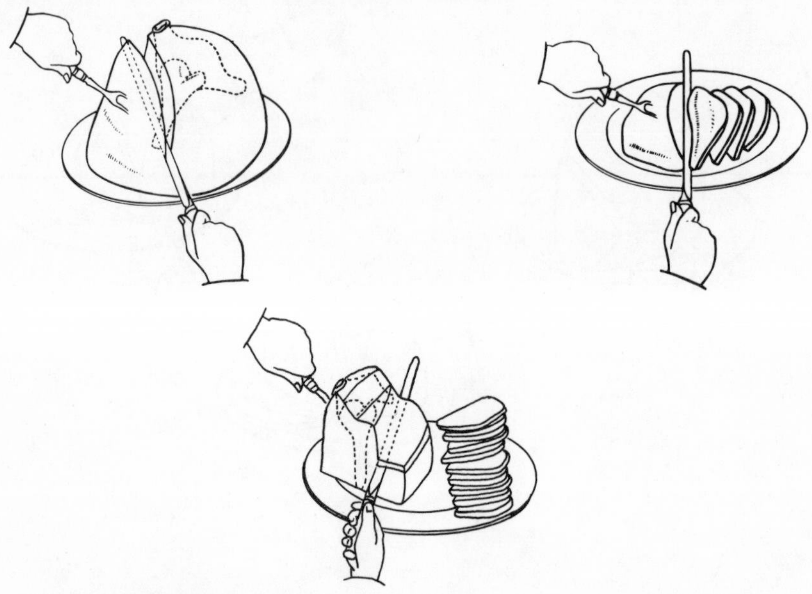

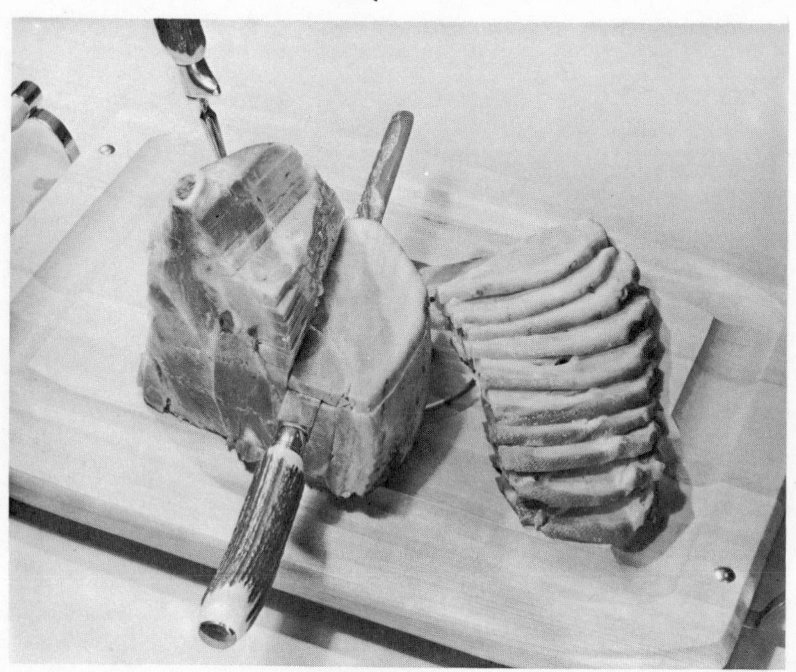

Make first cut toward the bone.

LAMB LEG ROAST

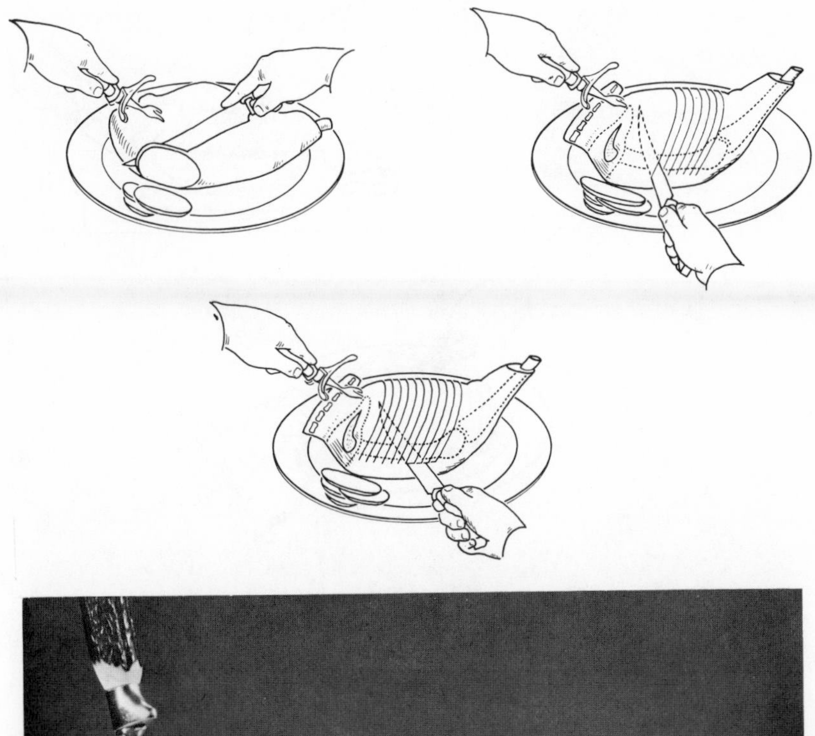

Cuffs add a decorative touch to the leg roast.

PORK LOIN ROAST

Pork loin roast carves easily on
plank placed in well of platter.

BEEF STANDING RIB ROAST

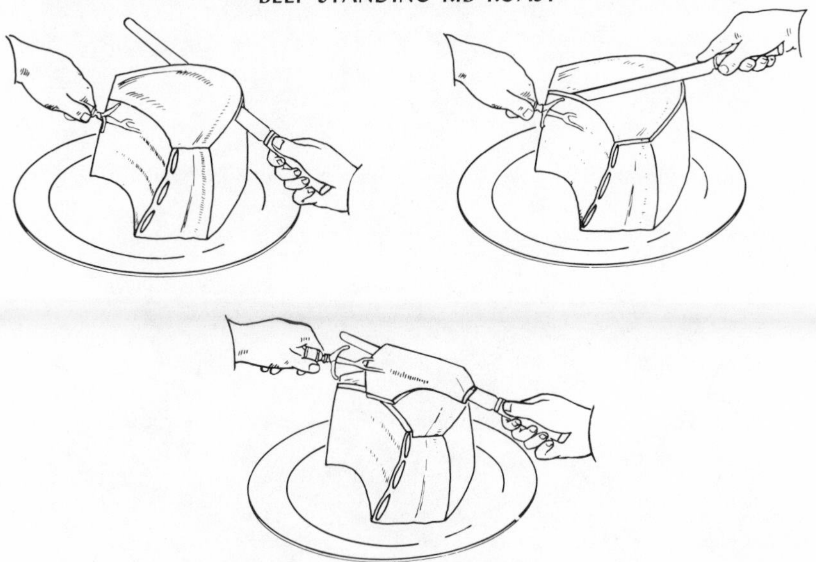

Roast Ribs of Beef — served rare, medium, well-done.

Roast Chicken. Plump, meaty, and roasted well-done, it carves easily using a steak set or small carving set.

Roast Rock Cornish Hens to Serve Six. Since no carving is necessary, serving spoons are the choice for serving.

Carving and Serving Other Poultry

Small Turkeys . . . Chickens

Use either the Side or Standard Style. (See pages 56 and 57.) A steak set or electric knife is the choice for carving. The drumstick and thigh are considered a serving portion and are usually served without further slicing.

Red Cornish Game Hens . . . Squab

The customary serving is one hen or squab. The larger sizes may be cut in half lengthwise, using poultry shears or kitchen shears if halved in the kitchen. The electric carving knife is another choice. If cut in half in advance of serving, the halves may be reassembled on the warm platter. Two spoons assist the host in serving the whole or half bird. (See page 52.)

Roast Duckling

Place bird breast up with legs toward left or right according to carver's convenience. The side toward the host is carved. The steak set is the choice for carving and serving at the table.

The structure of duckling is quite different from other poultry. The attachment of the wings and legs is so close to the backbone that it is sometimes difficult to locate these joints. The tip to host and hostess is to prepare for this in the kitchen. Place the roast bird back up on the cutting board. With point of knife cut through skin to loosen and free wings and legs by cutting into these joints. (See page 55.) Do not remove wings and legs. Place bird on warm platter breast up.

1. *Remove Wing.* Insert knife about one inch on the breast parallel to wing. Cut through crisp skin, turning knife slightly toward backbone to strike the wing joint. Complete the cutting to remove the wing, dropping it to the platter. The wing may not be served since the tip and first joint have little meat. The second joint may be set aside for second servings.
2. *Remove Leg.* Repeat this procedure to remove leg. Even though the release of wing and leg joints may have been made in the kitchen, it may be necessary to tilt the bird upward to make a clean cut. Transfer leg to side plate, then separate thigh and drumstick.

Roast turkey carves easily and quickly with the electric knife and two-tined fork.

Brace of Ducklings. Roasted, well-done, carving and serving at the dinner table are easy with a small carving or steak set.

3. *Remove Breast Meat.* Run knife close to keel bone. Turn knife slightly pushing downward to free meat from breastbone, lifting it off in one piece. Transfer it to side plate. Cut in half crosswise to make two pieces. Turn the platter or the bird on the platter and repeat the procedure to remove the second wing, leg, and breast meat.

A serving portion includes a piece of breast meat, a drumstick or thigh and a spoonful of dressing.

Roast duckling may be cut also in half, or quartered, usually in the kitchen before serving. The poultry shears, French knife, or electric carving knife may be used. The parts can be reassembled on the platter for serving.

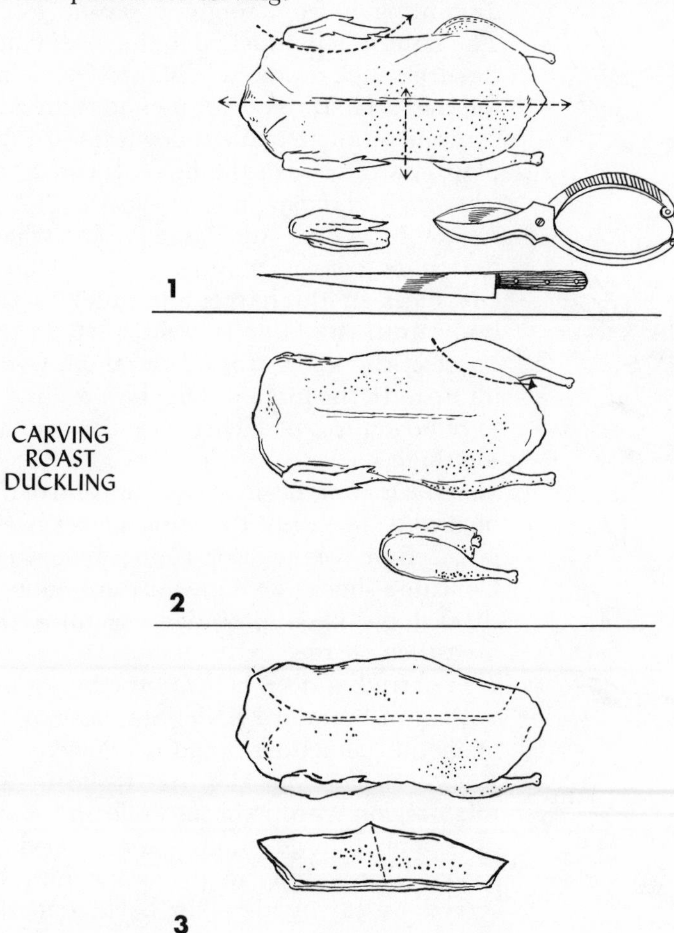

CARVING ROAST DUCKLING

Side Style

Carving Position. Place bird on its side, breast away from carver. Use this method also for carving half and quarter turkey roasts.

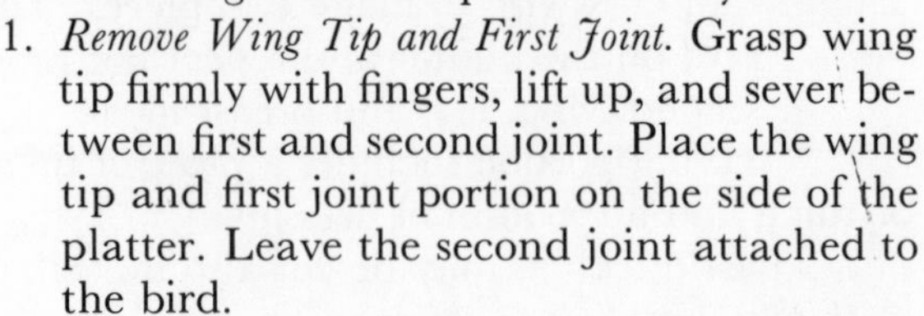

1. *Remove Wing Tip and First Joint.* Grasp wing tip firmly with fingers, lift up, and sever between first and second joint. Place the wing tip and first joint portion on the side of the platter. Leave the second joint attached to the bird.

2. *Remove Drumstick.* Grasp end of the drumstick and lift it up and away from the body, disjointing it from thigh or second joint. The latter is left attached to the bird. Place the drumstick on the side platter for slicing the meat. Hold the drumstick upright at a convenient angle and cut down toward the plate, parallel with the bone, turning the drumstick to make uniform slices.

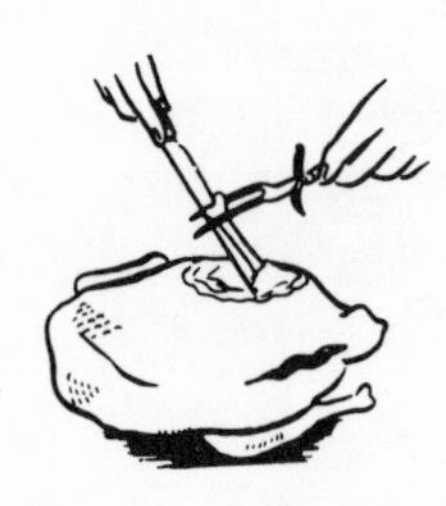

3. *Remove Thigh Bone.* Anchoring the fork where it is most convenient to steady the bird, cut slices of thigh meat parallel to the body until the bone is reached. Run the point of the knife around the thigh bone, lift up with the fork, and use fork or fingers to remove the bone. Then slice the remaining thigh meat.

4. *Slice White Meat.* Begin at the front end of the bird and slice until the wing socket is exposed. Remove the second joint of the wing. Continue slicing white meat until enough slices have been provided, or until the breastbone is reached.

   If preferred, a deep cut into the breast described in Standard Style, Step 5, may be made and directions 5 and 6 followed.

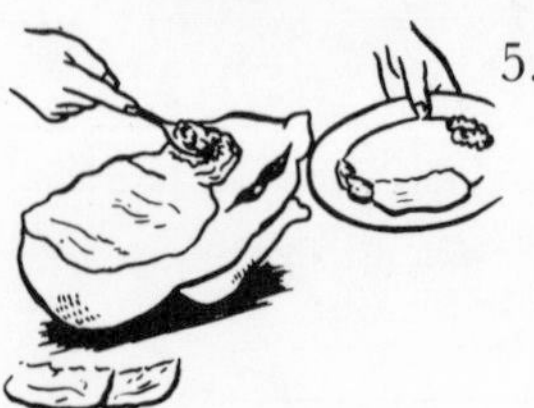

5. *Remove Stuffing.* Slit the thin tissue in the thigh region with tip of the knife and make an opening large enough for a serving-spoon. The stuffing in the breast may be served by laying the skin back onto the platter.

Standard Style

Carving Position. Place bird breast up with legs pointing toward right or left. A skilled, proud host may choose to carve the opposite side so that everyone can enjoy the exciting, mouth-watering process.

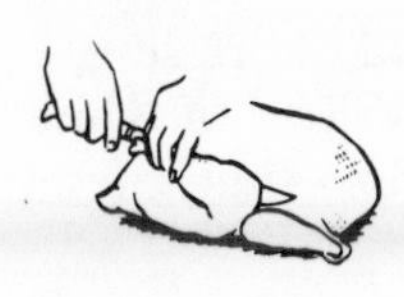

1. *Separate Leg* (thigh or second joint of drumstick). Hold drumstick firmly with fingers, pulling gently away from the body. At the same time cut through skin between leg and body following body contour with knife point.

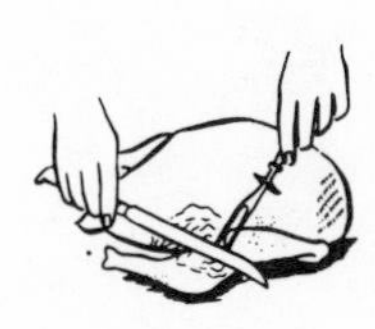

2. *Press Leg Away from Body with Flat Side of Knife.* Then cut through joint joining leg to backbone and skin on the back. Usually this joint snaps free assisting carver in completing separation of leg. With knife point follow body contour carefully to cut dark meat completely from the body.
   Hold leg on service plate with drumstick at a convenient angle to plate. Separate drumstick and thigh by cutting down through the joint to the plate.

3. *Slice Drumstick Meat.* Hold drumstick upright at a convenient angle to plate and cut down, turning drumstick to get uniform slices.
   The drumsticks and thighs of small birds are usually served without slicing.

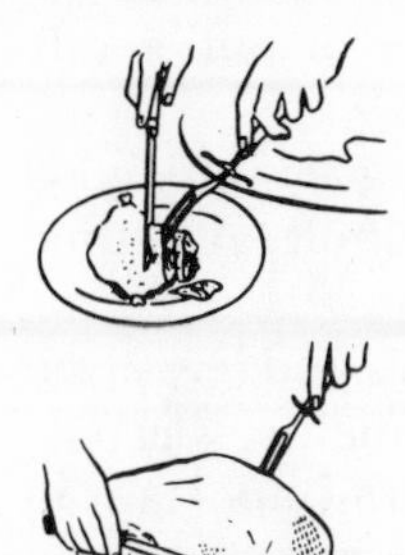

4. *Slice Thigh Meat.* Hold thigh firmly on plate with a fork. Cut slices of meat parallel to the bone.

5. *Cut into Breast Parallel to Wing.* Make a cut deep into the breast to body frame parallel to and as close to the wing as possible. This is an important basic cut. Continue as follows:

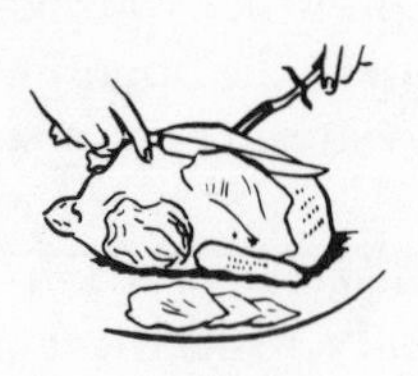

6. *Slice White Meat.* Beginning at front, starting halfway up the breast, cut thin slices of white meat down to the cut made parallel to the wing. The slices will fall away as they are cut to this line. Continue carving until enough meat has been carved for first servings.
   A serving includes a spoonful of dressing, a slice of dark meat and two slices of white meat. Gravy is best passed so that guests may help themselves.
   Remove stuffing from opening cut into side of bird where leg has been removed.

Imperial Style

What Is It? The roast bird is completely carved, then reassembled to retain much of its just-out-of-oven excitement, and ready to serve buffet style, or at the (family) table. (See pages 60 and 61.) The carving is done in the kitchen—ahead of time.

Service. For heating and serving choose a heat-proof platter on which to arrange the carved meat. An electric tray, designed especially for heating, keeping food hot, and serving, is another choice. Or, use the simple procedure of arranging the carved meat on a cookie sheet (or jelly roll pan) lined with heavy foil. Cover with a loose tent of foil for heating. To serve, lift carefully or pull gently onto warmed platter.

Carving Equipment. Use either the basic carving set, any good slicer with a two-tined fork, or an electric carving knife. A cutting board is a must.

In general, follow directions for removing wings and legs given in Side or Standard Style. Slicing technique of some parts is only slightly different, and bones and skeletal frame are important in reassembling the parts. Keep sliced meat and bones of each section together.

Transfer sliced white meat from cutting board, sliding knife under the slices and steadying with the hand to its position on frame. Then replace all remaining sliced meat, bones where necessary to fill in and support the meat as follows: sliced wing meat using first joint and connecting tip also, thigh meat, oysters, drumstick slices, then the drumsticks. Fill in with more stuffing. Replace any skin over its natural parts. Cover with a loose tent of foil. For oven reheating, allow 30 to 45 minutes. Remove foil tent, decorate drumstick ends as desired, garnish and serve.

Roast Turkey Imperial Style. Ready for the buffet or family dinner table.

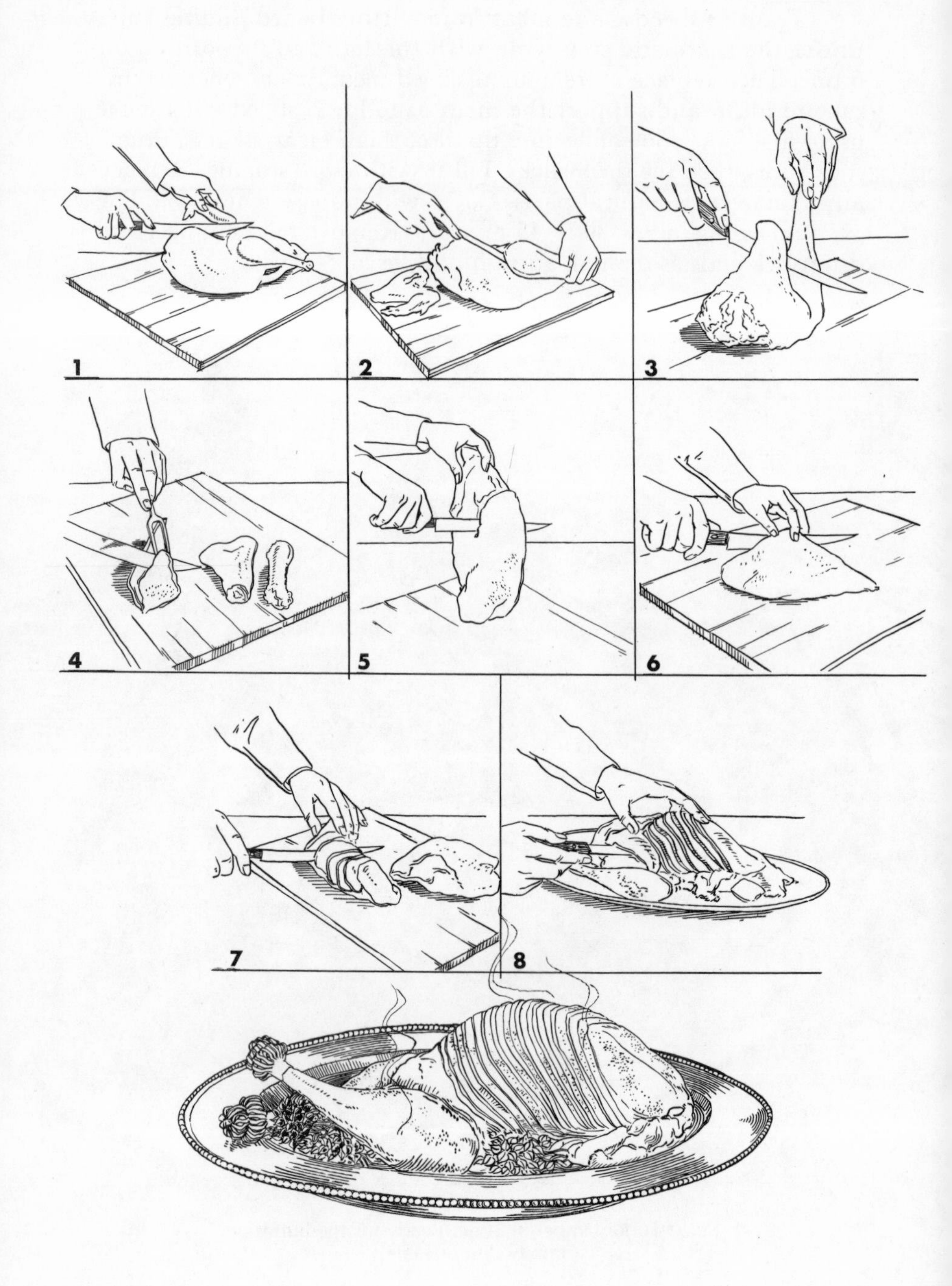
1
2
3
4
5
6
7
8

1. *Remove Wings.* Grasp wing firmly, place knife parallel to second joint about 1½ inches up on breast section. Turn knife at a 45° angle toward wing and cut down to strike wing socket joint. Complete cutting to separate wing completely. Separate meaty second joint from first joint and connecting tip. The latter has little or no meat. Set it aside for reassembling the parts. Slice white meat on the second joint. Repeat with second wing.
2. *Remove Legs.* Cut dark meat (thigh) completely from body following contour with knife tip. (See Standard Style—2)
3. *Separate Legs* into drumstick and thigh sections.
4. *Slice Thigh Meat.* If the crisp skin interferes with slicing, lift it off in one piece. Set it aside for later replacing it over its section. Place thigh bone-side up. Remove thigh meat in two sections, one from each side of bone. Set thigh bone aside. Holding each section securely with fork, slice thigh meat with knife at a 45° angle—2 or 3 slices from each section. Repeat with second thigh.

Drumstick Slicing. Hold drumstick at a convenient angle. Cut lengthwise slices on the cut side only, leaving the outside untouched. Repeat with second drumstick.

5. *Remove Breast Section.* Grasp back firmly as shown. Cut from center opening diagonally to wing socket. Repeat on opposite side. Grasp breast section firmly, lift up and back until wing socket joints snap separating it from the back section. Set back aside for second-day dishes, first removing the "oysters." The "oyster," one on each side underneath the skin, can be eased out with knife point from the spoon-shaped hollows on the back just above the thigh joint connecting leg to back.
6. *Separate Breast Meat* from its skeletal framework. Release each half, cutting closely along each side of the keel bone. Turn knife slightly, easing it downward under the meat and with cautious fingers lift the meat in one piece to the cutting board. Repeat with second half.
7. *Slice White Meat.* Cut each half into ¼ inch slices holding knife at a 45° angle.
8. *Assembling the Parts.* The heat-proof serving platter should be prewarmed. Since all of the stuffing may not be readily accessible, extra dressing should be planned casserole style.

Place the framework on platter. Some stuffing may be spooned onto platter first, or the back section, from which oysters were removed, may be placed first on the platter for a firmer base. Fill in around this base with more stuffing.

Chapter 8

SERVING CUES

"It's easier than you think!"

"In modern-day food service, science must be combined with common sense. Artistry must be tempered with practicality. Over all, graciousness and a spirit of warm hospitality should still rule, so in later years, memories of home will be centered around a gathering of family and friends at mealtime with good food and good cheer for all."—Beth Bailey McLean

Types of Service

In the past years there were only three types of recognized table service—the Russian, the English or Family, and the Combination of the preceding two. Today a fourth service has become a type of its own—the Buffet Service.

1. *Russian:* This service is considered the Formal Service. All food is served from the kitchen by attendants. No food is put on the table. Guests do not assist in serving. Food may be served in individual portions on individual plates, or it may be placed on large serving dishes (if necessary, separated into portions) for each guest to help himself. (See Chapter 9.)
2. *English or Family:* All food is served at the table by the host, the hostess, or both. (See Chapter 10.)
3. *Combination:* Usually the main course is served at the table. Soup or salad, or dessert, is served from the kitchen. A fruit cocktail is on the table when the guests enter the dining room. Unless the salad is served as a separate course, it is also on the table at the beginning of the meal.

4. *Buffet:* The food is attractively arranged on serving dishes and placed on a table or server. (See page 29.) It may be placed against a wall or be arranged as an island service. Guests form a line at one end, pick up their plates, and either serve themselves or are given servings from the main dishes by the host, hostess, or caterer. Guests take their meals to the area designated for eating. (See Chapter 9.)

Order of Service

For every type of service, except when guests are served at a buffet, the meal is first served to the hostess and continues around the table to her right up to the host. It then begins again on the left of the hostess, serving all on the left side. The host is served last. The hostess would do likewise in serving the dessert or beverage, except in reverse order, serving the guest of honor first, continuing on the left side of the hostess. She would then continue with the host, following along his left side and serving herself last.

Placing of Dishes

Dishes may be placed before a guest from either the right or the left. For convenience, the left side is preferred for food—the right side for beverages. Consequently, the general rule, "Serve and remove everything from the left except the beverage," has been widely accepted.

When a guest is served (formal service), the food must be served from the left in order to allow the guest to use his right hand conveniently. It is best to serve from one side as much as possible to avoid confusion.

If food is being served from the kitchen, two plates are brought in at one time. The plate in the left hand is served to a guest from the left side. The plate in the right hand is then transferred to the left hand and is served to the guest on the left, again placed from the left side. In serving the beverage (two cups of coffee being brought from the kitchen or serving table), the procedure is reversed. Serving takes place on the right side with the right hand.

Removing the Dishes

Remove one complete service (i.e., cocktail glass, plate, and spoon) with the left hand from the left side of the guest. Transfer it to the right hand and step to the setting to the right of the hostess (assuming that the hostess' service is removed first), and remove the next service with the left hand. Take the two services to a tray on the serving table. Continue until the tray is filled, then remove the tray to the kitchen. If more convenient, two services may be taken directly to the kitchen instead of to the serving table.

Removing the Main Course

1. Clear the table of food service first.
   a. Remove the meat platter and serving flatware to the kitchen.
   b. Remove vegetable dishes, gravy boat, bread tray, butter and relish dishes to the tray on the serving table. When it is filled, carry the tray to the kitchen. Take as many trips as necessary. If a serving table is not used, they may be taken directly to the kitchen.
2. Remove individual courses.
   a. Starting with the hostess, remove the main-course plate with the left hand from her left. Transfer the plate to the right hand to enable the removal of the salad plate or bread-and-butter plate with the left hand. Place it on top of the dinner plate. (When dishes are stacked behind the guests, it must be done as quietly and confidently as possible.) Proceed to the guest on the right, remove the salad plate, again with the left hand, and carefully place it also on the top of the plates in the right hand. Remove the dinner plate with the free left hand. This procedure removes two complete settings at one time. If the hostess waits on table, she removes her own plate last.
   b. If both salad and bread-and-butter plates are used, it is impossible to remove two settings at one time without danger of accident. If the setting is removed completely at one time, proceed as suggested above, taking the bread-and-butter plate in the free left hand instead of progressing to the second setting. Another method is to remove dinner and salad plates from two settings in succession as suggested above. Then returning to the first

setting, remove the bread-and-butter plate with the left hand, transfer it to the right hand and proceed to the next setting, removing the second bread-and-butter plate with the free left hand.

c. If, for some reason, the salad has been served on the right and the bread-and-butter plate is used on the left, only one setting can be completely removed at one time. The dinner and the bread-and-butter plates are removed from the left as suggested above, then stepping to the right, the plates are transferred to the left hand. The salad plate is removed with the right hand. Another method is to remove the dinner and bread and butter plates from two settings in succession. Then return to the right of the first guest, remove the salad plate with the right hand, transfer it to the left hand, and remove the second salad plate with the free right hand. Take the dishes to the tray on the serving table, stacking as many settings as can be gracefully handled. Take the tray to the kitchen, clear the tray, and repeat until the main course settings have been removed.

3. Salad Course—Served Separately.

a. When the salad is served as a separate course following the main course, remove the main course plate with the left hand from the left of the hostess and transfer it to the right hand. Proceed to the left of the person seated at the right of the hostess to remove the second main course plate with the left hand. Take both to the tray on the serving table or directly to the kitchen. The bread-and-butter plate is left on the table through the salad course.

b. To remove the salad course when it has been served as a separate course, remove the salad plate from the left of the hostess with the left hand, transfer it to the right hand, and remove the bread-and-butter plate with the left hand. Take the two plates to the tray or kitchen. Return to the guest seated to the right of the hostess and repeat, taking each setting to the tray or kitchen. If no bread-and-butter plate is used, follow the directions in 2b (above).

4. Remove salt and pepper shakers and any unused flatware to a small tray, which is covered with a tray cloth.

Crumbing the Table

Crumb the table where necessary, using a crumber or a napkin and small plate. This procedure may not always be practical when placemats instead of tablecloths are used.

Placing Additional Flatware

Following the crumbing, place any flatware needed for the dessert at each setting, or, if preferred, it may be placed on individual services. (See Beverage or Dessert Service below.) If the flatware is placed on the table, it is carried to the table on a small napkin-lined tray.

Beverage Service

1. Water glasses or stemware are filled to the three-fourths level before the meal is announced. Either of two procedures may be followed:
   a. Lifting the glass from the table with the right hand, fingers placed near the lower edge. Glasses are refilled behind the guests.

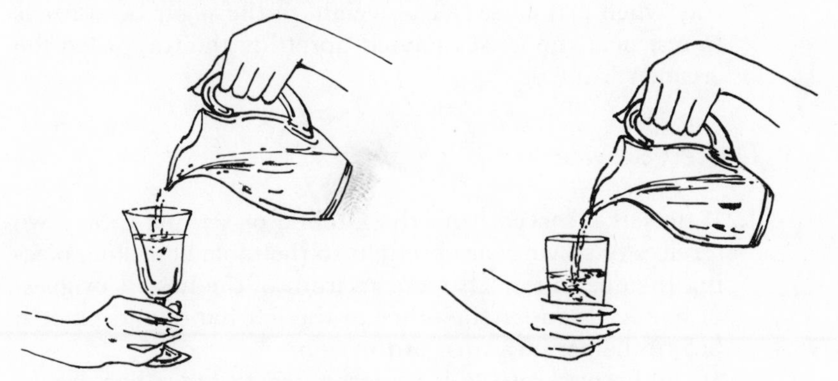

   b. Allowing the glass to remain on the table while filling it. In this case it is well to have a napkin in the left hand to blot drops of water which may stain the cloth. This method is convenient *only* if the distance between place settings is fairly large.

   The pitcher is refilled after every glass is filled and placed near the hostess on the table or on the serving table. To refill the glasses, they are passed to the hostess if the pitcher is placed on the table. If it is left on the serving table, the glasses are refilled by either of the methods mentioned for filling them.

2. If coffee or tea is served with the main course, two filled cups may be brought from the serving table or kitchen, placing one with the right hand at the right of the hostess (or guest of honor). The second service is transferred to the right hand and placed at the setting of the guest to the right of the hostess.
3. If served from the table, the complete service is placed on a tray in front of the hostess, or, if the tray is omitted, the coffee server is placed to the right of the setting, cups and saucers at the left with handles toward the hostess' right. Cream, sugar, and spoons are placed above the setting. The hostess moves one cup and saucer at a time to the center of her setting, pours the beverage, asks the guest's preference as to cream and sugar, and places a spoon on the right side of each saucer parallel to the handle of the cup. Spoons for the coffee may have been previously placed at each setting.
4. If sugar and cream are passed, it is preferable to use a tray. To avoid accidents, care should be taken in handling the tray when it is passed. The weight of the sugar bowl needs to rest near the wrist to avoid upsetting the tray when the creamer is lifted.

Dessert Service

1. If dessert is served from the kitchen or serving table, two services or servings are brought to the table at a time, placing the one in the left hand in front of the hostess or guest of honor. Transfer the other to the left hand, and place it before the person seated at the right.
2. If the hostess' setting is too crowded to place her dessert while she is serving the beverage, start the service with the person seated at her right and serve the hostess last.
3. If the hostess is serving the beverage from the table, the dessert may be served by the host. The host serves the dessert to the guest seated at the right of the hostess and so on to the right. If desired, the dessert flatware may be placed on each plate by the host just before it is passed.

Temperature of Beverage and Food

To serve any course at its best, all equipment must be either thoroughly warmed or chilled according to the food. Well prepared foods lose much of the palatability and zest unless the hostess definitely plans for keeping food at the proper temperature until eaten. Using the server or tea cart to hold appliances for chilling or heating foods has contributed to serving cold foods cold and hot foods hot.

Using the Server or Tea Cart

The server or tea cart ably assists the hostess in serving informal meals efficiently and conveniently. The extent to which it may be employed depends upon its size, the type of meal, choice of meal service, and space available in the dining area. The position of the server, whether it is placed on the right or left, will depend on its convenience to the hostess and its relation to the kitchen and electric outlets.

Types of Service Made Possible with the Use of the Server or Tea Cart

1. The server may be used for bringing the entire meal into the dining area. Each course is removed in turn from its shelves and served. Dishes and all service from completed courses are passed by each guest to the hostess who places them on the server. This service is adapted only to a small group. A multi-shelf server is necessary for efficiency.
2. It may be used as a service table to which each course is removed prior to being wheeled to the kitchen. The next course is placed upon the cart and wheeled back.
3. It may be used for the service of courses at the table usually served by the hostess. If electrical appliances are used, it offers an opportunity to use them in the serving or dining area.
4. It may be used to relieve what might otherwise be a congested serving area. If used in conjunction with the main course, the person sitting to the left of the host may assist him by serving the vegetables and the gravy. It may also be used at the left or right of the hostess for the beverage and dessert service.
5. It may be used as a serving table for rolls, butter, candies, nuts, relishes, cream, and sugar.

Chapter 9

AN INFORMAL DINNER . . . without paid service

"Entertain and enjoy it!"

"The barbecue in the backyard, the toasted sandwiches by the fireplace, the kitchen table buffet and the meal-on-a-tray carried to the patio are expressions of the modern homemaker's emancipation from formal customs."—Beth Bailey McLean.

Within the limits of good taste, today's homemaker may extend her imagination to entertain as informally as she chooses. For her everyday pleasure, she may wish to creatively experiment with the preparation of informal family dinners; when entertaining intimate friends, she may find the Sunday night supper on the patio or serving in front of a blazing fire relaxing; for the neighborhood get-together she knows the appetizing buffet is enjoyable to all; and for the festive occasion, the semi-formal dinner is most gratifying.

Informal meals do not mean charm and hospitality are sacrificed, neither do they imply careless food service. On the contrary, appreciation and admiration of how food is prepared and how attractively it is served are more keenly observed and freely expressed in an informal atmosphere than in the formal food service where employed help is available to assist the host and hostess. The success of a dinner is not dependent on the type of service used but rather on the hospitable and gracious attitude of the host and hostess which permeates the atmosphere during the dinner hour.

Come Over—It'll Be Buffet

One of the easiest and most delightful ways to handle a large or small dinner party is the buffet service. It may be as informal as an after-game snack or as elaborate as a wedding reception. A table displayed with well prepared, beautifully served food is an inviting picture, even to those whose appetites may be numbed.

In planning the buffet meal, a few "rule-of-thumb" suggestions are appropriate regardless of the type of table service used.

1. The most attractive buffet tables offer well-balanced menus with a variety of colors, textures, and tastes of food.
2. The table appointments (china, glassware, flatware, and linens), together with the centerpieces and food, combine to present a harmonious, appetizing setting. Just as an artist does not present his painting without a suitable frame, so food should be served in appropriately designed dishes. Borders are meant to enhance the contents of the platter. Patterns, containers, and garnishes should enhance, not compete with, food displayed.
3. If a round dining table is used for the buffet, it will be most attractive and convenient if used as an island, approachable from all sides. The entree, if placed in the center and elevated to improve its accessibility, will achieve a place of distinction and may also serve as the centerpiece.
4. The tea cart or a side table may be used to provide additional space for serving beverages if the buffet table will not amply provide space for them.
5. Wherever possible, it is best to provide tables and chairs to accommodate the guests. "A lap-eater's life is not a happy one." If tables or space for tables is not available, a considerate hostess will provide lap trays or TV table trays.
6. A gracious hostess will serve only easily managed food (fork-tender foods, with little liquid) so as to facilitate ease in transferring the food to a table or in eating the food if the lap-tray style of service is used.
7. Plates and trays, if they are used, are placed where they are readily accessible to guests as they approach the table. The menu needs to be kept sufficiently simple so each guest needs only one plate. (See page 29.)
8. The place setting of flatware, the napkins, and beverage are best placed as the last items to be picked up if separate tables have not been provided with place settings previously arranged. (See page 29.)
9. The food is placed to the right of the plates and follows all around the table or down the length of the table. Sauces, dressings, and garnishes are placed near the food with which they are to be eaten.
10. The serving flatware is placed on the table near each serv-

ing dish at the beginning of the meal. The handles are placed parallel to the edge of the table with sufficient space around them to provide an easy grasp.

Types of Table Service

A. Sit-Down Buffet

1. Dining table is set as though the meal would be served at the table.
   a. Necessary table appointments are at each place setting.
   b. Water glasses are filled.
   c. Salad plates are at the place settings, or the salads may be served from the buffet table.
   d. Appetizers are placed at each setting unless they have been previously served.
2. Guests serve themselves at the buffet table after they have enjoyed the appetizers.
   a. Tables are cleared while the guests serve themselves.
   b. Water glasses are refilled.
3. Guests return from the buffet table.
   a. Beverages other than water are also served at the table.
   b. After the main course, the tables are cleared to a tea cart or side table.
4. Dessert is served from the kitchen, at the buffet table, or guests serve themselves from the buffet.

B. Card Table Buffet

1. Dining table is used for the buffet service. If space is needed for the placement of card tables, the dining table may be moved against a wall.
2. Card tables placed in the dining and living room areas will provide a congenial atmosphere if the space is large enough to accommodate guests and tables comfortably. When space is at a premium, the tables may also be placed in adjoining rooms to avoid discomfort of a congested area.
3. Folding chairs are more correctly scaled to the height of card tables and will therefore be more comfortable than the normal dining chair.

4. Place cards may be used to insure seating arrangements if the party is large, or be used to direct guests to the tables.
5. As with the sit-down buffet, the tables are set as though the meal were to be served at the table with the appetizer at each setting if it has not been previously served. The procedure of self-service and clearing of the tables is also comparable to that of the sit-down buffet.

C. TV Table or Tray Buffet

TV Table Trays or Lap Trays which are sturdy in structure, ample in size, and attractive in design have become important accessory items for entertaining in unusual areas. Interest in an exceptional television program, fascination for the glowing embers in a hearth, the opportunity for pool-side relaxation or even the discomfort of smoke-saturated air around a grill have welcomed the mobility and versatility of tray service. Equally important is the convenience of using trays where space in living accommodations does not allow for any other type of service.

Lining the trays with colorful placemats of fabric, paper, or other interesting textures helps to achieve an attractive tray service, as well as contributes to the functional qualities of a tray. Placemats reduce slippage of table appointments and serve as silence cloths, as well as protectors to the surface of the tray.

The tray buffet, the most casual type of meal service, responds beautifully and effectively to the wishes of a creative hostess.

Dinner Is Ready

Since breakfast in the average family may be a hurried affair, and luncheon less carefully planned and executed because some of the family members are not present, serving the family dinner, or the meal to which guests have been invited, needs to be given special consideration if it is to be done in a relatively relaxed and informal manner. Ideally, dinner in every family should become an activity which family members or guests will anticipate with pleasure during the routine of the day's work.

The following step-by-step procedure of serving a dinner to the family and to friends may serve as a guide to successful informal entertaining:

Mrs. Smith has invited four guests to a six-thirty dinner, Mr. and Mrs. A and Mr. and Mrs. B. Mr. A is district manager for the manufacturing concern in which Mr. Smith is employed. Mr. B is a college friend of the Smiths. The dinner is planned for the Smith family and guests, totaling eight. Carol Smith is a sophomore at the university, and Charles Smith is an eighth grader in junior high school. Carol and Charles have been trained from childhood to help with the household tasks. They have learned to handle dishes and to serve food with dexterity and finesse. Their responsibilities have also given them a critical eye for setting tables correctly. Flatware, glassware, and other table accessories have never been allowed to stray from the spot where each belongs. They have learned one standard that would pass the most rigid test of any occasion.

Mrs. Smith has always made an effort to plan her work so that she may greet her guests upon their arrival without a look of fatigue and anxiety. She begins to prepare for the dinner several days in advance. In her early experiences as hostess she found it necessary to plan everything with paper and pencil. Now she refers to several standardized menus, which have proved to be successful through trial, error, and improvement. Any of them may be modified to suit such varying conditions as cost, season, diets, and tastes of her guests. From her files, she has chosen a three-course menu and, with one or two changes, has decided to serve the following:

Melon Cocktail

Fillet of Beef - Mushroom Sauce - Potatoes O'Brien
Buttered Asparagus - Lettuce-Tomato Salad - French Dressing
Dinner Rolls - Jelly

Peppermint Ice Cream
Cookies Coffee

As a hostess without employed service, she has learned that the best choice for the first course is a cold food, since it does not lose its palatability during a slight delay after the announcement of dinner before the guests take their places. For the dinner course, much of the preparation can be done in advance, as can be seen by examining Mrs. Smith's schedule. Last-minute preparations have been avoided in this menu. Even some "trailers" (the mushroom sauce) can be made in advance and last-minute flurries avoided. For the dessert, only the coffee needs to be prepared at the last. She will have the coffee and water measured for the coffee maker in advance, to be started later during the progress of the dinner.

Having decided upon the food to be served, Mrs. Smith uses her twenty or more years of experience to follow a certain routine. Her method of planning has given her a comfortable satisfaction that she is completely ready to be an unharrassed hostess. She has learned that the success of a detailed plan is determined to a great extent by the organization of meal preparation.

Planning for Dinner Preparation*

Two days before or earlier

1. Look up linen and other table accessories.
2. Take inventory of food supplies.
3. Make out market order and order supplies.

Day before

1. Melons - wash and ice.
2. Potatoes - boil in jackets.
3. Meat - prepare for roasting.
4. Salad greens - wash and ice.
5. Cookies - mix and refrigerate.
6. Ice cream - soak peppermint candy in milk.
7. Rolls - set dough.

Dinner Day

1. Shape rolls.
2. Slice and bake cookies.
3. Prepare casserole of potatoes for oven.
4. Prepare mushroom sauce; leave in double boiler.
5. Prepare butter pats for table.
6. Prepare cocktail; set to chill.
7. Peel and marinate tomatoes.

*Some of the food—rolls, ice cream, and cookies—might be purchased. Decision depends on (1) time available for preparation, (2) quality of food purchased outside the home, (3) cost of foods, (4) hostess' skill in preparation, (5) available freezer space for foods prepared in advance or purchased.

8. Measure water and salt needed for frozen asparagus into saucepan.
9. Assemble china, linen, flatware, etc.
10. Finish making ice cream.
11. Set table (Carol).

Planning for Table Appointments

Linen

1 tablecloth
8 napkins
2 extra napkins
2 tray cloths*

Glassware

8 water glasses or stemware
8 fruit cocktail glasses
1 water pitcher**

China

8 plates - under cocktail glasses
8 dinner plates
8 salad plates
8 dessert plates (same as cocktail plates)
7 cups and saucers
1 deep small bowl
1 large platter
1 medium platter
1 gravy boat
1 casserole
1 plate for bread
1 creamer and sugar bowl**
1 plate for cookies**
1 plate for extra butter**

Flatware

15 teaspoons
8 dinner forks
8 dinner knives
8 salad forks (dessert)
8 butter spreaders
2 serving spoons
1 gravy ladle
1 jelly spoon
1 butter knife**
1 ice cream knife**
2 serving spoons**

Miscellaneous

1 carving set
2 pairs salt and pepper shakers
1 jelly dish
1 coffee server
1 trivet**
1 large tray**
1 small tray, lined with tray napkin**
1 plate and napkin for crumbing**
Centerpiece

*Desirable though not essential under rolls and cookies.
**On serving table.

Seating Arrangement

CHARLES MR. B MRS. A

MOTHER FATHER

MR. A MRS. B CAROL

SERVING TABLE

KITCHEN DOOR

Individual Place Setting

1. Plate with Fruit Cocktail; 2. Knife; 3. Teaspoons; 4. Salad Fork*; 5. Dinner Fork; 6. Napkin; 7. Bread-and-Butter Plate**; 8. Butter Spreader; 9. Butter; 10. Water Glass; 11. Beverage Cup with Dinner or Dessert Course.

*On serving table.

**Salad plate serves as bread-and-butter plate.

The Dinner Table

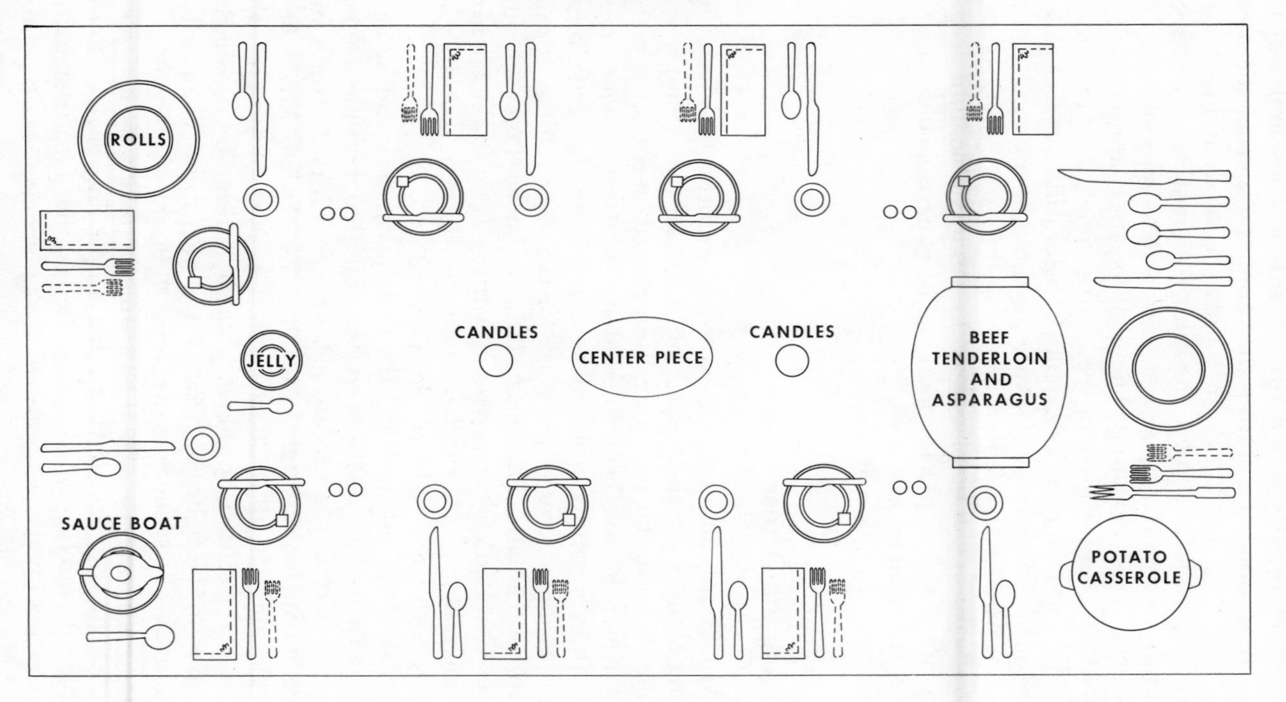

Immediately after lunch Mrs. Smith will assemble all the equipment necessary for setting the table and serving the meal. Carol has the responsibility for preparing the salads and for setting the table. She will also tend to the dining-room details. This gives Mrs. Smith an opportunity to rest during the afternoon and prepare leisurely for the evening. The final food preparations will be started while Carol is busy in the dining room. The individual place settings will vary to this extent: Charles will have two glasses (one for milk). The serving flatware for the dinner course will be arranged at Mr. Smith's setting. Dishes and flatware marked** on diagram (page 78) will be placed on the serving table until needed thus leaving space for placing food or dishes necessary during the serving of the meat course.

Serving the Dinner

When Mrs. Smith announces the dinner and leads the way into the dining room, the fruit cocktail and salad for the second course are on the table. Butter pats have been placed on the salad plates and water glasses have been filled. Jelly compote is placed near Mrs. Smith. The family positions have not been changed. In extending the table to give ample space for the place settings at each side, Carol and Charles have been shifted to the end on each side. This gives Carol an excellent position with relation to the kitchen, the serving table, and her father since she will be responsible for the serving with Charles' help. (See page 78.)

The family members may take their positions standing near the back of their chairs. This gives Mrs. Smith opportunity to ask Mrs. A to be seated in a very simple manner: "Mrs. A, won't you be seated at Mr. Smith's right? Mrs. B at Carol's left? Mr. A here at my right and Mr. B at Charles' left." As Mrs. Smith gives the signal for being seated by the very act of sitting down, Charles quickly steps to the right and assists his mother to her chair before seating himself. Everyone is seated from the right of his chair.

Mrs. Smith gives the signal for eating by taking up her spoon for the cocktail, eating it slowly so that ample time is given to the guests to eat leisurely. Carol watches her mother for the signal to remove the salad plates when her mother places her spoon permanently on the service plate on which the cocktail glass has been placed.

1. *Carol:* Removes salad (left hand—left side) and water glass (right hand—right side) from her father's place setting to the serving table. Their removal will make room for serving the main course dishes. To eliminate this step Mr. Smith's salad and water glass might have been on the serving table at the beginning of the meal.
2. *Charles:* At same time, starting with his mother's setting, removes her cocktail glass and service plate (left hand—left side), transfers it to his right hand, and removes Mr. A's cocktail glass and service plate with his free left hand (left side) and carries the two services to the kitchen. He continues around the table to the right. To avoid accidents, it is necessary for Charles to have a firm hold at the foot of the cocktail glass and the plate. If the plates are needed for dessert, he may rinse and wipe them after he has cleared all the settings.
3. *Carol:* Brings eight hot dinner plates to the serving table, placing four in front of her father (left side—both hands). The remaining four are left on the serving table until needed. She returns to the kitchen to bring the large meat platter holding the meat and the asparagus. The platter is placed above the dinner plates (left side—both hands); returning to the kitchen she gets a tray holding the potato casserole, mushroom sauce, and plate of hot rolls and places it on the serving table. The casserole is then placed to the left of her father, and the rolls and sauce are placed to the left and right of her mother. (See page 79.)
4. *Mr. Smith:* Carves the meat (see Chapter 7) and serves both meat and vegetables after he has carved sufficient portions of meat. He passes the plate to his right stating distinctly that the first plate is for Mrs. Smith. The second plate served goes to Charles, and so on to the right. Then beginning with Mr. A he serves those sitting on his left. He serves himself last.
5. *Carol:* Replaces father's salad and water glass. If the meat course needs to be kept warm, she removes the platter and the serving bowls to a warming tray on the serving table or a warming oven in the kitchen. Carol removes carving and serving tools lest they be damaged by the heat. The latter may be quickly washed and wiped ready to be returned to the table for second serving use.
6. *Mrs. Smith:* Helps herself to mushroom sauce and passes it to Mr. A saying, "This is mushroom sauce for the meat. Won't you help yourself and pass it?" She does likewise with the rolls and the jelly.

7. *Mr. Smith:* Observes the guests' need for replenishing their food. Carol watches for the signal to return the meat platter and vegetable bowl to the table. Father carves additional servings of meat before offering any to the guests, or Carol may have carved the necessary portions in the kitchen before returning the platter to the table. When he is ready, he says, "May I serve you, Mother?" Mrs. Smith answers, "Yes, thank you," and definitely indicates whatever she desires. If she states no preference, Mr. Smith gives her a small serving of each food.
8. *Mr. Smith* asks, "Mr. A, may I serve you?" and so on around the table to the left. Then serves those to the right down towards himself.
9. *Carol:* Serves additional butter, if necessary, from an extra supply on the serving table.
10. *Charles:* Catching signal from his mother to remove dinner plates, he starts with his mother's setting (left hand—left side) transferring it to the right hand; then removes salad plate (left hand) placing it on the dinner plate; steps to Mr. A's left, removes his salad plate (left hand) which he places on the first salad plate. Lastly, he removes Mr. A's dinner plate (left hand —left side) and takes both settings to the kitchen. He repeats this same procedure around the table to the right.
11. *Carol:* Removes the meat platter (with the serving tools) from the dining table (uses both hands from the left of her father) and carries it to the kitchen. She then removes the casserole, roll plate, sauceboat, and jelly and places them on the tray on the serving table. The tray is then carried to the kitchen.
12. *Carol:* Removes salts and peppers to a small tray. Places it on serving table.
13. *Carol:* Does any necessary crumbing with empty plate (left hand) and folded napkin (right hand) from left side starting with her mother's setting.
14. *Charles:* Refills water glasses.
15. *Carol:* Places flatware for serving dessert at her father's setting (left side).
16. *Carol:* Places eight dessert plates (both hands) at her father's right.
17. *Carol:* Places platter with molded ice cream in front of her father (left side—both hands).
18. *Carol:* Places tray with cups and saucers to the left side of her

mother. (Handles of cups face to the right as they stand in front of Mrs. Smith).

19. *Carol:* Places the coffee server on trivet or tile to the right of her mother (right hand). Places cream and sugar in center of table near her mother.
20. *Mr. Smith:* Serves dessert, the first going to Charles and so on around the table. Mrs. Smith will be served last. (See 22 below.)
21. *Carol:* Places plate with cookies between her setting and Mrs. B's setting.
22. *Mrs. Smith:* Serves coffee. First cup goes to Carol and so on around the table to the right. Then she begins with Mr. Smith on her left, and completes serving those on the left.
23. *Mrs. Smith:* Helps herself to cream and sugar, passes each to Mr. A and so on to the right.
24. *Carol:* Removes the dessert platter and serving flatware, as well as the tray with coffee server to the serving table after the dessert and coffee have been served.
25. *Carol:* After being seated, takes the cookie plate, and passes it to the right.
26. *Mrs. Smith:* When this last course has been completed, Mrs. Smith places her napkin, casually folded, at the left of her setting. Waiting a moment for a lull in the conversation, she suggests retiring to the living room. She rises from the right of her chair (with Charles' assistance) and leads the way into the living room, thereby concluding the meal.

Chapter 10

A SEMI-FORMAL DINNER
. . . with paid service

"Spare the hostess and spoil the guests."

The informal dinner party, though hospitable and enjoyable, does not create an appropriate setting for all occasions. On the other hand, the truly formal dinner with its butlers, maids, and its extensive finery in table appointments continues to be acceptable only by the society which still maintains large homes with all the dramatic formality which complements their spacious and regal décor.

The semi-formal dinner (often referred to as "formal" dinner) is a blend between the relaxed atmosphere of the informal and the elegant atmosphere of the formal. This service has become fashionable for special occasion dinners and festive entertaining.

The menu used by Mrs. Smith for the informal dinner has been employed as follows to show how the same food may be adapted to a different type of table service.

Melon Cocktail
Fillet of Beef - Mushroom Sauce - Potatoes O'Brien
Buttered Asparagus Dinner Rolls
Jelly
Lettuce-Tomato Salad
French Dressing Swedish Wafers
Peppermint Ice Cream
Cookies Coffee

Planning for Table Appointments

Linen

Tablecloth
Dinner napkins
Extra napkins*

Glassware

Footed goblets or tumblers
Cocktail glasses
Cocktail glasses (ice cream, if it is not served in slices)
Jelly dish (silver, crystal, or china to match)
Water server

Flatware

Teaspoons (cocktail)
Teaspoons (coffee)
Salad forks (if salad is separate course)
Dinner forks
Dinner knives
Dessert forks or spoons
Jelly spoon
Extra flatware*

Miscellaneous

Tray with tray cloth (creamer/sugar)
Centerpiece

China**

Plates (cocktail service - 8″ or 9″)
Salad plates
Wafer tray (if salad is separate course)
Bread tray (rolls)
Cookie tray
Cups and Saucers
Creamer and sugar

Serving the Dinner***

At the semi-formal dinner, food is served to each member of the dinner party by the butler or maid. No food is passed at the table since neither the host nor hostess assists in serving. Each guest has all the necessary service within comfortable reach.

The semi-formal service is similar to the informal in that the hostess or guest of honor may be served first. If there are two persons serving, they both start the service at the same time. It is well to plan that each maid has at least eight guests and not more than twelve guests to serve during the meal.

*Extra napkins and extra flatware are provided on the serving table to meet emergencies.
**In the formal dinner there is no bread-and-butter plate.
***Adapted from the Russian Service, Chapter 8, page 63.

In the semi-formal type of service, food may be served on the plates in the kitchen and the plate placed on the table before the guest, or an empty plate is set at the place setting and each person is served individually from bowls or serving trays. In the case of the latter service, the serving tray, presented to the left of a guest, is held on a napkin in the palm of the maid's hand unless the tray is too heavy or awkward and needs the right hand to help support it. Care should be taken in presenting it to a guest to hold it conveniently low. (See page 88.) If the food is arranged on a serving dish, the proper spoon or fork must be with it.

All food in the semi-formal type of service, except accompaniments to courses, is arranged on individual service plates. In neither formal nor semi-formal service are second servings, except rolls, offered.

Order of Table Service

The degree of formality practiced with meals considered "semi-formal service" depends to some extent on the size of the group being entertained. The following guides for serving pertain to several group sizes: Letter "a" refers to service designed for small, intimate groups. Letter "b" refers to service designed for large, banquet type groups.

1. *Cocktail Service*
   - a. The cocktail is served after guests are seated. Bring two cocktail services (cocktail glass and service plate) from the kitchen. Place one before the hostess or guest of honor (left side—left hand), transfer the second from the right hand to the left, and place it before the guest seated to the right of the hostess or guest of honor.
   - a. Remove one cocktail service (left side—left hand). Transfer it to the right hand. Hold the foot of the cocktail glass and plate in such manner that there is no danger of accident or noise. Proceed to the person seated to the right of the hostess and remove the second cocktail service (left side—left hand). Take to the kitchen. Continue removing two at a time until all are removed.

     When taking out the last two services, return with two filled dinner plates. Serve guests in the same manner and in the same order that cocktails were served.
   - b. The complete cocktail service is on the table at the time guests enter the dining area.

b. Remove one cocktail service with the left hand and transfer it to the right hand. Go to the person seated to the right and remove the second cocktail service (left side—left hand). Place the two services on a tray on the serving table. Repeat until the tray is filled, not stacked. Carry the tray to the kitchen. Continue the same procedure until all settings are cleared.

When returning to the dining table after taking the last tray to the kitchen, bring back four filled dinner plates, again using a tray. Place them on the serving table. Take two at a time to the table. Serve each guest in the same manner and in the same order as cocktails were served.

2. *Rolls*

a/b. Serve rolls, one guest at a time, after the dinner course has been served to all guests (left side—left hand). This serving tray is also held on a napkin in the palm of the hand.

Serve rolls, to one guest at a time, from the left side.

3. *Salads* . . . with main course
   - a/b. Place the salad on the table *before the guests are seated.* If no beverage is served with the main course, it may be placed either at the left or right side of the place setting.
   - a. The salad may be served *after the main course* has been served to each guest. The maid brings two at a time and serves each guest from the left with the left hand, or if no beverage is served, it may be placed on the right side served with the right hand.
   - b. The salad may be served *after the main course* has been served to each guest. The maid then brings a tray of salads to the serving table from which she serves two guests at one time (left side—left hand), or if no beverage is served, it may be placed on the right side served with the right hand.
4. *Salads* . . . separate course
   - a/b. Serve the salad in the same manner as 3-a or 3-b, with the exception that the salad is placed in the center of each place setting (left side — left hand). Wafers or crackers which accompany salads are offered in the same manner as rolls are served. (See page 88.)
5. *Clearing the Place Settings* . . . after main course
   - a. Remove the dinnerware, one setting at a time (left side —left hand). Transfer to the right hand. Remove the salad plate with left hand. Carry the setting to the kitchen, or, if more convenient, to a tray on the serving table; then remove it to the kitchen.
   - b. Remove two settings at one time by removing one dinner plate (left side—left hand). Transfer it to the right hand. Remove the salad plate (left side—left hand) and place it quietly on the dinner plate. Proceed to the guest at the right, remove the salad plate (left side—left hand) and place it carefully on the first salad plate. Remove the dinner plate (left side—left hand). Take to tray on serving table. Continue to remove settings till the tray is filled. Carry to kitchen. Repeat procedure until all place settings are cleared.
6. *Removing Salt and Pepper Shakers*
   - a/b. Remove the salt and pepper sets, from the most convenient position, to a small tray covered with a tray cloth. At the same time remove the unused flatware from each setting, from whichever side it is placed at the setting.

7. *Crumbing the Table*
   - a/b. Remove crumbs and other dry food particles from the table wherever necessary, using a small napkin and plate. Work from the most convenient side of the guest, holding the plate in the left hand. A crumber designed for this purpose may also be used.
8. *Dessert Service*
   - a/b. Place any flatware needed for the dessert to the right side of the setting. Use a small tray to carry the flatware to the table. A tray cloth will prevent flatware from slipping.
   - a/b. Bring four dessert services on a large tray from the kitchen to the service table. Carry two desserts at one time to the guests at the table, placing the dessert in the center of each setting (left side—left hand).
   - a/b. After each guest has been served, offer the accompaniment (cookies) from a tray in the same manner suggested for rolls. (See page 88.)
9. *Coffee Service*
   - a. After the dessert and cookies are served, coffee cups are filled at the serving table, two cups at a time as each pair of guests is served. The coffee cup is placed to the right of the setting with the right hand. Sugar and cream are offered from a serving tray (left side—left hand) after everyone has been served coffee.
   - b. If the service is hurried and a large number are being served, the cups and saucers may be on the table at the beginning of the meal or placed when the dessert is served. The cups are then filled by the maid from a large coffee server.

     Another method for serving beverages is to bring filled cups and stacked saucers on a tray from the kitchen to the serving table. Each maid is responsible for carrying a sufficient number on the tray for the guests she serves. Two cups are then placed on the saucers, brought to the table, and placed in the usual manner (right side—right hand). Cream and sugar may be offered, or, if they are on the table, they are passed by the guests.
10. *Completion of the meal*
    - a/b. As in the informal meal, when the last course has been completed, the hostess, Mrs. Smith, places her napkin at

the left of her setting, waits for a lull in conversation, then suggests leaving the table.

An after-dinner beverage graciously extends sociability in the more relaxed setting of the living room or patio.

INVITATION
12
6

Chapter 11

MANNERS— EVERY STEP OF THE WAY

". . . and a good time was had by all!"

Invitations

A. Whom to invite?

Inviting guests who know and enjoy one another will naturally result in pleasure-filled hours. Introducing new faces, however, may add a new sparkle of interest and add a change of pace to the party. Experienced hostesses give careful consideration to the guest list and hasten to add that the "magic" of successful entertaining is the careful planning which begins with the invitation list.

A few simple questions such as these will help to create compatible groups:

1. Will the guests have a common conversational threshold? Combining guest lists to meet two social obligations with guests of dissimilar interests may be a tragic social blunder. For example, if a group of social friends together with business acquaintances were invited to the same gathering, you may find them to be conversational strangers to each other. In this case, it may be better to give two parties.
2. Is there a pleasant balance between friendly, enthusiastic individuals and those who are friendly, but conservative?
3. Is there a balance in numbers between women and men, adults and children?
4. Will your guests enjoy each other? Social friction leads to a strained rather than congenial atmosphere and should be avoided whenever possible.
5. Will the number of people invited be entertained comfortably in your home or on your patio?

B. When to invite?

The first act of consideration towards dinner guests is to extend an invitation at least a week ahead of your party to provide time for guests to make necessary arrangements to enjoy your hospitality. Another courteous act is to time the dinner, insofar as possible, to the convenience of the guests.

C. How to invite?

1. Invitations for informal entertaining may be given by informal note, by telephone, or by visiting card; formal entertaining requires a formal note.
2. Invitations are given in the name of the hostess or host/hostess.
3. Special care should be taken in stating the date and exact hour or hours, especially if given verbally. The important thing to remember is whatever the form of invitation, a guest should be told everything necessary to know.
   a. In many instances, it becomes necessary to give detailed directions to locate your home or apartment.
   b. When formal dress is expected for the occasion, it may be simply stated on the printed invitation as "Black Tie," indicating that dinner gowns or formal cocktail dresses and men's dinner coats are to be worn. If a choice of formal or semi-formal clothing is appropriate, the invitation reads "Black Tie Optional." This indicates that women's dress then ranges from a dinner gown to a simply designed costume, and men's attire ranges from dinner coats to business suits. For the casual occasion "Sportswear" indicates casual apparel. These notations would appear in the lower right hand corner of the invitation opposite R.S.V.P.
   c. When dinner is to be followed with entertainment outside the home, the activity should be stated.
   d. When dinner is given in someone's honor, the invitation makes mention of it.
4. Invitations require thoughtful and immediate acceptance or declination. It is considered a serious breach of manners, unless for a very good reason, to cancel an invitation after it has been accepted.

Arrivals and Introductions

A. Responsibility of Guests

1. Plan for arrival five minutes prior to time designated by the hostess. It is as inconvenient for the hostess to have early arrivals as it is to have latecomers. Minutes before the set dinner hour may be precious to the hostess for completing last minute preparations for her guests. On the other hand, the minutes lost because of late arrivals may contribute to a "less-than-excellent food" which the hostess has carefully prepared. A gracious hostess will wait fifteen or twenty minutes for a guest but need wait no longer.

   If a dinner guest is late, he or she briefly apologizes to the hostess on arrival. At a later opportunity a more detailed apology may be given the hostess. If the latecomer is a woman, the hostess rises; if a man, she may remain seated. The hostess acknowledges the apology by shaking hands with the guest and saying something to put him at ease. The serving of the meal for the belated guest may start at the beginning unless he is considerate enough to say, "Just let me begin with this course."
2. Participate in conversation by contributing interesting topics of discussion. Monopolizing conversation is a serious social offense.
3. Know and use good manners at the table as well as in social circles. It is this "finished ease" which helps you to meet others with self-assurance. Today's increased opportunities for broader education through many educational and news media prohibit claiming the excuse of bad manners on the basis of lack of opportunity to learn.
4. At a large private party the host and hostess may not find it possible to see that formal introductions are made with everyone. Therefore, feel free to introduce yourself to anyone near you even though you may not have been formally introduced.

B. Responsibility of Host/Hostess

1. The hostess has the responsibility of initiating most of the activities of the group, especially meal activities.
2. The prime duties of the host are to concern himself with the comfort and pleasure of the guests.

a. A gracious host will be ready to greet the guests at the entrance to bid them welcome. Latecomers to a small, informal group, are introduced by the host to the guests at the table. At a larger, more formal dinner, introductions are limited to only a few guests, with general introductions being deferred until guests have reassembled in the living room.
b. The host will give special recognition to the needs of guests of honor or newcomers in a group.
c. The host will assist the hostess wherever possible to ease her efforts and make her entertaining an enjoyable event.

3. The host and hostess will share the responsibilities of entertaining as a team. When he is involved with details of serving, the hostess will give more attention to conversation. Whereas, when she is busy with serving rituals, he in turn will be responsible for conversation.

C. Participation of the Young Family Member

Children who appear briefly at a party may make a delightful contribution. They often can be helpful in passing canapes, showing guests where to put their wraps, directing the parking of automobiles, etc. Such service would give them a sense of importance and belonging.

Dinner Is Announced

A. Seating

1. If there is no paid service, the hostess informally makes her own announcement of the meal. It may be as simple as, "Won't you come to dinner?"
2. The hostess enters the dining area first in order that she may direct the seating of her guests. She is accompanied or followed by the oldest person present or one to whom honor is being shown. It is a gracious gesture for members of the family to respond to the dinner invitation by taking other guests to the dining table. The use of such phrases as, "May I take you to dinner?" or "Won't you go to dinner with me?" are acceptable.
3. Place cards are used for formal functions, for informal ones if a large group is to be seated, or when they contribute to

the decorative scheme for the special occasion meal. Place cards are placed above the plate at the center of the setting or on top of the napkin.

4. The guest of honor is the oldest person present or someone whom you wish to honor. The man guest of honor is seated at the right of the hostess, the woman guest of honor at the right of the host. Guests second in importance are usually seated at the left of the hostess and host.
5. In seating her guests, the hostess directs them from her chair with cordial and dignified phrases such as, "Won't you be seated at my right, Mr. J--?" or "Mrs. J--, please be seated next to Mr. W--."
6. Each member of the dinner party remains standing behind his chair until the hostess is seated. If the chairs have been placed so that the line of the tablecloth is not broken, there will be ample room for being seated without the necessity for many adjustments of the chairs when being seated.
7. It is an expected courtesy for each man to draw out the chair for the woman who is seated at his right. A gentleman not only assists a woman in being seated but also assists her when she rises to leave the table. If there are only women present, this courtesy is sometimes shown by the

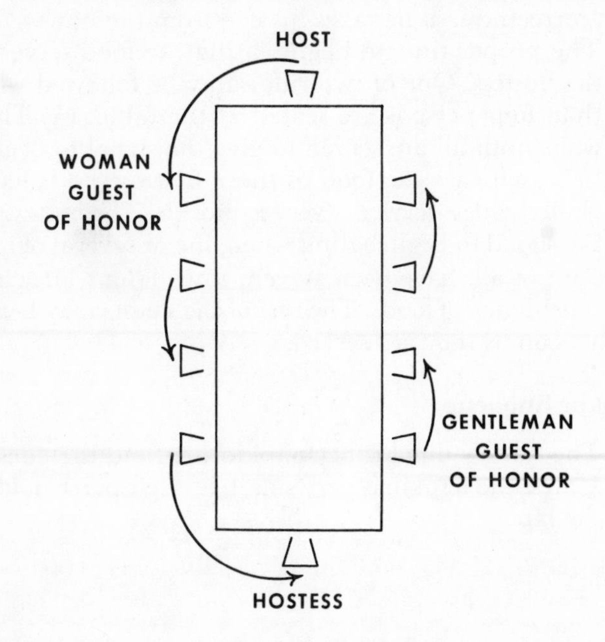

younger members for the older members of the group. There is no set rule as to which side of a chair should be approached when seating oneself. However, if gentlemen are to assist ladies at their right, it would reduce confusion if all approaches, assisted or unassisted, would be made from the right of the chair.

8. One is correctly seated at the table when the body is erect but not rigid. The feet are placed squarely on the floor in front of the chair or the ankles crossed gracefully, not wrapped around the legs of the chair. Heels should not rest on the rungs of the chair. Sit well back on the seat of the chair not on the edge.
9. The blessing may be asked before being seated or just before the napkin is lifted from the table after being seated. When everyone is seated, conversation should cease. To save any guest embarrassment, the hostess, without delay, should ask the host or honored guest to "ask the blessing."

B. Beginning the Meal

1. The hostess in all cases sets the pattern and pace of mealtime activity. She is the first to unfold her napkin, to choose the silver she wishes to be used. A guest need never doubt "correctness" if he takes his cue from the hostess.
2. The proper time to begin eating the food served rests on the hostess. One of two rules may be followed when more than four persons are seated at the table: (a) The hostess waits until all are served to give the signal to begin eating, in which case the food of those first served is likely to be chilled unless service is very rapid. (b) The hostess may give the signal to begin eating when one or several of her guests, but not all, have been served, since long waits change the consistency of foods. The rest of the guests may begin eating as soon as they are served.

C. Napkin Etiquette

1. The hostess unfolds her napkin first and the guests follow. Unless the napkin is very small, it is left partly folded across the lap.

2. The napkin is used inconspicuously at all times. Unfold the napkin below the level of the table. Except to lightly blot lips, the napkin is left on the lap until the close of the meal.
3. At the end of the meal, the hostess and others members of the family may refold or casually fold their napkins and place them beside their plate, thus suggesting that the dinner party retire to another conversational area. Unless a guest remains for another meal, his napkin is not refolded but placed casually folded to the left of his place setting. Paper napkins, like fabric napkins, are left partially folded.

D. Knife and Fork Etiquette

1. If in doubt as to which piece of flatware to use for a certain course, take your cue from the hostess.
2. When knife and fork are used together to cut bite-sized pieces, several customs are acceptable. (See page 2.)

   a. American Custom

   In the United States it is customary to lay the knife across the top of the plate well toward the right after food has been cut into one bite size. The fork is then transferred from the left to the right hand, conveying the food to the mouth with the tines up.

   b. Continental or European Custom

   The fork is kept in the left hand while eating the food that has been cut, conveying the food to the mouth with the fork held tines down.

   In either custom, the fork is held in the left hand near the top of the handle with the prongs downward and pressing firmly into the food. The index finger is placed on the shank so that it points to the prongs and is supported at the side by the thumb. The end of the fork handle is held well within the palm. The other fingers close underneath, holding the handle tightly.

   The knife is held firmly in the right hand exactly as the fork is held in the left, with the end of the handle well in the palm and the index finger pointing down the back of the blade. It is used to cut food that cannot be cut with a fork.

3. When using the fork alone to cut food, hold it, prongs up, between the thumb and forefinger as in eating vegetables. By turning the wrist, food may be cut by pressing down with the left edge of the fork. In an effort to be firm, caution needs to be taken against shaking the table or raising the elbow for leverage.
4. Upon finishing a course, lay the knife and fork side by side, near the center of the plate, the blade of the knife turned toward the center of the plate. The handles are on the right side, resting on the plate edge with the tines of the fork up. The fork is left nearer the center of the plate.
5. When two forks are used, a dinner fork and a salad fork, the salad fork may be left on the salad plate or placed on the dinner plate parallel to the dinner fork. This facilitates removal of the place setting if the complete cover is removed at one time.
6. When passing the plate for a second helping, place the knife and fork parallel to one another towards the upper edge of the plate, with handles resting on the plate edge. Once a piece of flatware has been used in a course, the handle must not again touch the table. It is ill bred to tilt flatware against the rim of the plate with the handle on the tablecloth as this may result in food dropping on the cloth.
7. The individual butter spreader is placed on the bread and butter plate when the place setting is laid, and it remains there throughout the meal. Its only purpose is that of spreading bite sizes of rolls, breads, or crackers.

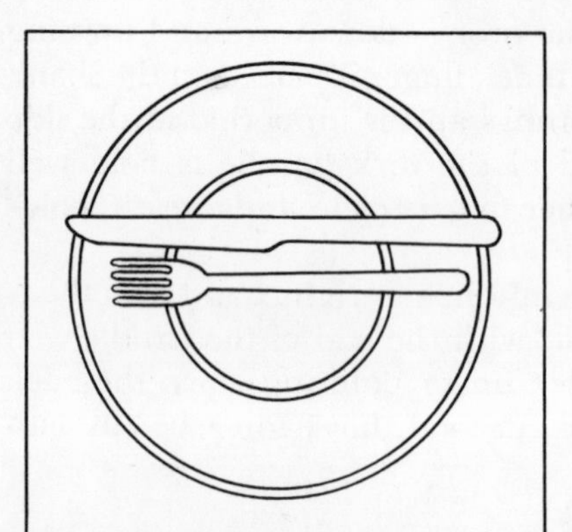

Placement of knife and fork at end of meal.

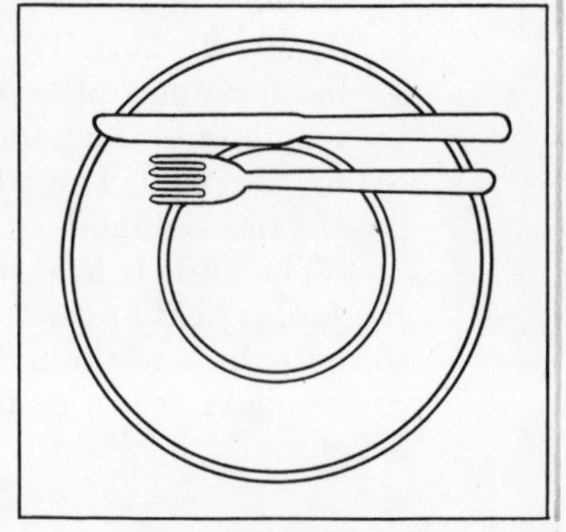

Placement of knife and fork when passing plate.

E. Spoon Etiquette

Regardless of what food is eaten with a spoon, only the amount which can be eaten with one bite should be spooned at one time. Sipping or nibbling from the spoon a bit at a time is unattractive and considered discourteous.

1. Spoons are supplied for tea, coffee, chocolate, and clear soups but are used largely to test temperature and flavor. After that the spoon is laid on the saucer, and the beverage is drunk from the cup or glass.
2. The spoon used with the cocktail or sherbet glass, beverage cup, or anything with a saucer or a service plate underneath should be placed on the saucer or service plate. The spoon is never left standing in the glass or cup when not in use.
3. An ice served with the meat course is eaten with the dinner fork. (This necessitates serving an ice that is frozen hard just after the dinner has been served). If the hostess has furnished a spoon for a soft ice or frappé, use it. If there is no plate under the ice, the spoon must be left on the dinner plate when not in use.
4. For desserts that have an accompanying juice or syrup (compote of fruit, fruit tarts, shortcakes, meringues), both a spoon and fork may be used. For stewed fruits this double service is especially convenient, for the fruit pits may be easily separated from the fruit by using both.
5. Ice cream and sherbets may be eaten with a spoon, a dessert spoon, or a salad fork, or with a small round fork especially designed for that purpose.
6. In eating soup from a plate or cup, fill the spoon two-thirds full, dipping it away from you. Sip from the side of the spoon, not from the tip. Eating from the tip under any circumstances results either in a strained wrist motion or in projecting the elbow out too far from the body, thus giving an awkward appearance. Do not tip the soup plate to get the last drop of soup. Do not break crackers into the soup; rather, leave them on the bread-and-butter plate, eating them as a bread. Croutons are eaten in the same way unless they are very small and have been put into the soup as a garnish. Drink bouillon served in cups after it has been tested for temperature with a spoon.

Fill the soup spoon two-thirds full, dipping it away from you.

7. The spoon for soup or cereal is permitted to lie in the plate or bowl until the food has been eaten; then it should be placed on the service plate.

The How's of Eating Various Types of Foods

. . . The faultless finesse of fine manners begins at home . . .

A. Fingers? Spoons? Forks?

Foods may be classified in the general categories of "finger foods," "spoon foods," or "fork foods," depending on their texture and consistency. Olives, celery, and all similar foods are transferred from the serving dish to one's own salad or bread-and-butter plate with a pickle fork or with fingers when serving silver is not supplied. Finger foods are eaten from one's own plate—never from the serving plate.

B. "Lest We Forget"—Accepted Eating Practices

1. *Apples* are pared, if preferred, cut in small sections, and eaten with fingers or fork.
2. *Artichokes* (French) are eaten from the fingers, taking off leaf by leaf and dipping them into the sauce. The bottom, or heart, is broken and eaten with a fork.
3. *Asparagus* is eaten with a fork.

4. *Bacon* may be eaten with the fingers, if crisp. If not crisp, it is more conveniently eaten with a fork.
5. *Bananas* are peeled from the top down, cut into small pieces, and eaten with a fork. Sliced bananas with cream are eaten with a spoon.
6. *Bread* is broken into bite sizes and buttered as each piece is eaten. It is never buttered in the whole slice. If jelly or other accompaniment is used, it is handled the same as butter. Bread and its accompaniments are placed on a small plate provided for the purpose—either the bread-and-butter plate or the salad plate.
   Hot breads (muffins, cornbread, biscuits) are an exception to the practice of spreading each bite as it is eaten. "Take two, butter one," a well loved invitation of the Southland, meaning "take two and butter them while they are hot" may be observed if the hostess extends the invitation. Hot breads, like other breads, are broken into bite sizes before eating.
7. *Butter* is placed on the plate (bread-and-butter plate or salad plate), never directly on food when taken from the butter tray. Honey, jams, or conserves are treated in like manner. If a meat accompaniment is served, it is placed on the dinner plate next to the meat and eaten with the meat with a fork.
8. *Cocktails* such as oysters and shrimp are eaten with a cocktail fork. A fruit cocktail is eaten with a spoon.
9. *Corn-on-the-cob* is eaten by holding the cob at one end in the fingers of one hand. It is not served for formal occasions. It is more easily handled if it is broken or cut into short lengths before serving it at the table. It is buttered with the regular knife, resting one end of the cob on the edge of the dinner plate.
10. *Olives* are eaten in small bites while held with the fingers. The pit is placed on the plate after the olive has been eaten.
11. *Peaches* are quartered, the stones removed; the quarters may be peeled, if preferred, before eaten with a fork. They may be cut in halves and eaten with a spoon after the stones are removed. The European way is commendable, though it requires a skill. The fruit is held in place on the plate with the fork and then peeled with a knife, never touching it with the fingers. Bits are cut off with the knife and eaten with the fork.

Apples may be pared and cut in small sections and eaten with fingers or fork.

Bread is broken into bite sizes and
buttered as each piece is eaten.

12. *Potato—Baked.* A fork is used to remove the potato or to eat the potato from its shell. Many people prefer to have the potato left in the skin while eating. If the potato is not served split with a lump of butter inside, or if more butter is desired, it is taken from the bread-and-butter plate and pressed into the potato with the fork. The skin may be eaten if desired.
    Potato Chips are eaten with the fingers.
    Potatoes—French Fried are eaten with a fork, whether crisp or soft, since either is coated with an oil.
13. *Poultry* is usually not eaten with the fingers in the presence of guests at a semi-formal or formal dinner. As much of the meat as possible is cut from the bone, and the remainder is left on the plate. Fried chicken that is not greasy may be eaten from one hand at an informal or casual meal.
14. *Salads* may be cut with a knife and eaten with a fork when served as quartered head lettuce or similar salads where greens, vegetables, or fruits are in large segments. Today, salad greens are eaten in entirety, rather than treating them as merely a garnish.
15. *Sandwiches,* unless a small, party size, are broken in half no matter how difficult the procedure. Club sandwiches, as the barbecued sandwich, are a meal in themselves and are eaten with a fork. The knife may be helpful in some cases.
16. *Seeds, skin, or bones.* If it is necessary to remove such inedible portions from the mouth, do so as unobtrusively as possible, using spoon, fork, or thumb and forefinger to convey them to the plate. The use of a napkin to hide the procedure usually calls attention to it. If a fruit sauce, such as prune sauce, contains large pits, the pits are removed in the dish before taking the fruit to the mouth.

    If seeds or fine bones lodge in the mouth, resulting in discomfort, leave the table to dislodge them. Using a toothpick, the tongue, or, even less desirable, the finger in the presence of others is extremely discourteous and very objectionable.

In Case of An Accident

If an accident occurs at the table, a good hostess will remain calm and unruffled, regardless of what happens at the table or in the kitchen. If there is service, ignore the accident as much as possible and let the maid take care of it. If there is no service and the accident necessitates attention, do what is necessary as inconspicuously as possible. As a guest, do not make excessive apologies to your host or hostess when an accident occurs. Make apologies quietly and make them brief. Wait until an opportunity comes later to speak with your host or hostess.

Conversation

1. Conversation at the table should be cheerful and pleasant and of such a nature that everyone may take part in it. No one should monopolize it. A hostess will try to introduce topics of conversation that will invite the "too-quiet" guests to enter into conversation. Conversation should be divided between the person at the left and the one at the right. It is not polite to visit with one person to the embarrassing exclusion of the other. The hostess might consider placing two good talkers as she would two bright lights. Two brilliant minds need to be placed opposite each other in order to include others in their general conversation. Children, according to their ages, can and should be encouraged to contribute to the conversation. Unpleasant or controversial topics should be avoided. The basic aim of hospitality is to offer warmth, cheer, and good will.
2. Loud talking and laughing or anything that attracts undue attention to one's self or a group at a table are not complimentary to well-poised individuals.
3. Neither host nor hostess should make apologies for any part of their hospitality even though they may be experiencing an uneasiness.
4. Consideration for people on special diets should be given by appearing oblivious to any differences and by avoiding any references to them. Likewise, the person following a special diet avoids discussing choices at the table.

Passing, Serving, and Second Helpings

1. *In passing any food at the table,* be careful not to rest fingers near or within the food. If the dish has a handle, turn the handle toward the person who is about to take it from you.

2. *In accepting a dish passed to you,* if convenient, use the left hand so that the free right hand can be used immediately for helping yourself without shifting the dish. Where both fork and serving spoon are to be used, both your left and right hand should be used. In this case, the person to the left holds the serving platter or bowl for you.
3. *If asked to pass food,* place the serving flatware in the dish, if there is any, and pass the dish to the one next to you. The hostess may say, "Help yourself to ________ and pass it." Only in that case may you help yourself first.
4. *When pouring from a cream pitcher,* try to pour steadily and bring the pitcher sharply to an upright position so that cream will not run down the side of the pitcher. If the liquid begins to run down, there is nothing to be done to prevent it from soiling the table linen. It is very improper to use your napkin or flatware to stop it.
5. *When a host or hostess offers to serve a second helping* at the table, the use of the terms "more" or "second helping" should be avoided. Instead, use forms as "May I serve you ______?" or "Let me give you ____" or "Won't you have hot coffee?"
6. *If you do not care for a course,* you should not refuse it unless you have been given that choice. Tea or coffee, for example, may be refused. Receive all other dishes and eat what part of it you can. If you must leave it untouched, do not give the impression of being neglected or ill-provided for but pay a little more attention to the conversation so that those around you may not notice.
7. *If your preference for a food is consulted,* courtesy requires that you express some preference *promptly* whether it matters greatly to you or not. Refusal to express a preference may be embarrassing to your host and hostess.
8. If you wish to take the last helping of any *food that may be offered* or passed to you, it is proper to do so. Refrain from expressing looks as if you doubted the supply.

Personal Habits at the Table

Small rules of behavior, daily nurtured at family meals, become a tower of strength for your ego when you go out among friends on social occasions. What type of image do you reflect on yourself and on your family?

1. *Do you avoid bending to your plate* as you raise your fork in an effort to convey food to your mouth?
2. *Do you use wrist motion in using silver* instead of awkward elbow motion?
3. *Do you employ both hands in eating?* If you do not keep one hand or the other in the lap a good part of the time, it appears as if you were in a great hurry to finish the meal, or were very hungry.
4. *Do you cut all the meat on your plate at one time?* Prepare each bite as it is eaten unless preparing a child's meal for him.
5. *Do you tip a plate or glass* to obtain the last drop of its contents? Avoid the "good-to-the-last-bite" appearance.
6. *Do you avoid cooling* beverage or food by blowing on it?
7. *Do you avoid looking over the top or rim of cup or glass* while drinking? *Do you avoid gulping a beverage* as though you were parched?
8. *Do you remember to blot lips lightly* before drinking to avoid leaving marks of greasy lips on the rim of glass or goblet?
9. *Do you use your hands gracefully* in handling the handles of silver or cups? Avoid the exaggerated ways as curling the little finger or holding a cup or glass with both hands.
10. *Do you eat slowly* enough to finish one bite before taking another?
11. *Do you eat the food you have placed on the fork or spoon immediately* after you have taken it? Never hold the food, especially near your mouth, after the food has been picked up. It should be eaten promptly or left to rest on the plate. Do not suck food, such as ice cream, during your conversation.
12. *Do you talk before food has been swallowed?* If the amount of food taken is not so large, a brief delay to answer a question will scarcely be noticeable.
13. *Do you choose to ask to have things passed* rather than to reach for anything normally out of reach? It is discourteous to extend hands or arms across or in front of another's place setting.
14. *Do you remember to use the serving silver* provided to remove food from the platter or serving plate rather than your own?
15. *Do you refrain from picking a dish up from the table while eating* from it?
16. *Do you toy with* salts and peppers, napkin rings, silver, or other *small items* between courses or during the meal?

17. *Do you turn your head from the table* if it is necessary to use a handkerchief? Do you use it as quietly and as unnoticeably as possible?
18. *Do you restrict reading at the table* to the time when you are alone? Since the enjoyment of one's meal is greatly increased through fellowship, reading is not a desirable mealtime activity.
19. *Do you avoid handling your face and hair* when dining or serving at the table?
20. *Do you avoid smoking at the table* unless ash trays are provided? The hostess indicates her approval of smoking at the table by providing ash trays, and therefore guests may not assume that she merely forgot them. Dinnerware is never substituted for an ash tray.
21. As a hostess, *do you gauge your eating time to the speed of the dinner guests?* The hostess needs to be especially alert so as not to appear to bring the meal to a close before the guests have finished. No person at the table should complete the meal conspicuously before the rest.
22. As a guest, *do you appear totally unconscious of the host's or hostess' efforts in serving,* especially if the host is experiencing some difficulty in carving? Come prepared to introduce an interesting discussion or relaxing conversation during their activity, so as to put them at ease.

The Use of the Finger Bowl

The use of the finger bowl is not necessarily an "affected" after-meal ceremony, but rather it may serve as a delightful convenience to end a meal where difficult finger foods, as lobster, have been served. The water will be slightly warm, and after a seafood course, a slice of lemon floating in it will serve as a pleasant skin freshener.

The fingertips, one hand at a time, should be dipped into the tepid water and dried lightly *on the napkin* while dipping fingers of the second hand into the water. Fingers are always dried on the lap, never above the surface of the table.

At a formal dinner, finger bowls may be brought on before the dessert course. The finger bowl will be on a doily on a service or dessert plate and may be flanked by the dessert flatware. It is the guest's responsibility to set the flatware at each side of the plate and transfer the finger bowl with the doily to the upper left of your place setting.

A finger bowl may be provided after any course which would deem its use necessary or convenient.

Leaving the Dining Room

1. *The hostess takes the initiative in leaving the dining room.* Usually a few words such as, "Let us have more comfortable chairs in the living room," will avoid long, awkward moments at the table after the last course has been finished.
2. *It is proper for guests to leave* at any reasonable time after dinner unless some form of entertainment has been mentioned.
3. *Guests, on leaving,* should *express their appreciation* to the host and hostess. They may take leave of such guests as are standing near the hostess, but it is unnecessary to make a special effort to say goodnight to others.
4. It is considered *good form to express gratitude again* for hospitality enjoyed within two weeks. If one is leaving town, a note of appreciation should be written; otherwise, a telephone call is proper.
5. *Guests are accompanied to the door.* If convenient, the door is held open until guests have gone out of sight. Unescorted women guests are accompanied to their cars or taxis by the host or any other male guest at the party if the host is occupied.

APPENDIX

A LITTLE MORE ABOUT CARVING EQUIPMENT AND KITCHEN TOOLS

Carver's Helper: a two-tined fork identified by the extra width between the tines, and its shorter overall length compared to the carving knife, meat slicer, and steel. It helps to hold large roasts and boneless rolls firmly and prevents the roast from sliding and turning during the slicing.

Electric Knife: one of the newer tools also referred to as an electric carving and slicing knife. It is available with cord and cordless —the latter is operated by rechargeable batteries. The blade(s) are virtually permanently sharp. The technique for use is easily mastered and consists of learning to guide the blade(s) through the meat or poultry.

French Knife: a useful tool for chopping, dicing, mincing, shredding and slicing of foods. It is easily identified by a characteristic shape. The blade near the handle is quite wide. The cutting edge of the blade curves near the point so that the knife can be used with a rocking motion holding the point firmly to the cutting board. Different blade lengths are available.

Poultry Shears: a tool formerly called "game scissors" operates as a pair of scissors. Its two blades are slightly curved to a point and are short with one blade having a serrated cutting edge and a notch near the "pin" holding the blades together. It may also have a steel spring for greater cutting power which is readily removable for washing. Poultry shears are available as a part of a carving set or in all steel, with or without the spring.

Steel: the sharpening tool used by the carver and chef to true the cutting edge. A steel is easily identified by its characteristic shape and overall length. Although a definite technique for its use is required, it can be readily mastered. A steel is available as part of a carving set or separate tool. It may be used at any time the carver or chef considers it necessary to renew the edge for perfect slicing. Its use is the dramatic touch in the dining room or at a buffet in contrast to the whetstone more conveniently used before serving.

Whetstone (hwet′ stōn′): an abrasive stone (carborundum) for sharpening knives and other edged tools. It can be, and often is, the only sharpening tool used, or its use may be followed by finishing the edge with the steel.

A LITTLE MORE ABOUT TABLEWARE

Centura (sĕn to͞o rȧ): "A tableware made of one kind of Pyroceram glass-ceramic." It is available in several designs. It resists breaking, chipping, cracking, crazing. "Centura cook-serve pieces" can be used for top-range cooking, in the freezer, as well as for serving.

Dirilyte refers to another choice of tableware, "The original golden-hued flatware and holloware which started out as Dirigold in Sweden . . ." This solid alloy has a distinctive gold color and a characteristic hardness. As Dirilyte, it is made in this country and is available in several patterns. It can be monogrammed.

Flatware and Holloware: the terms for two types of tableware for eating and serving food. They replace the terms "silver" and "silverware" since tableware is available today in sterling silver, gold leaf plated sterling silver, plated silver and stainless metals —the latter include alloys and stainless steel.

Flatware refers to the pieces used by each person—knives, teaspoons, cereal or soup spoons, forks, salad forks, etc. It also includes serving spoons, pickle fork, salad servers, jelly spoons and sugar shell.

Holloware refers to the pieces such as bread and roll plates, casseroles, coffee and tea pots, trays, salt and pepper sets, candlesticks, etc. A modern trend in flatware and holloware is the use of pearl, bone, stag or wood to form the handles.

Hollow handle refers to the larger handle of the knife so designed for firm gripping. Today hollow handles are standard style for the knife and the butter spreader.

Nambé Ware (Näm′ bā): A solid alloy of eight metals "handcrafted" originally in Mexico and now in southwestern United States. It is presently available only in holloware. The color is a beautiful silvery gray. Each item is individually cast in a sand mold. It is heat, cold, freeze, scratch and crack resistant. Nambé is the name applied to a group of Tanoan people occupying a pueblo in New Mexico.

Pyroceram (pī rō ser ăm): General term for Corningware — A special glass-ceramic produced for kitchen and dinnerware adapted to cooking, freezing and serving. Its unique non-porous texture is virtually break, chip and crackproof. This glass ceramic withstands extremes in temperature.

Vermeil (vehr māy) is considered precious tableware, developed in France during the eighteenth century. A special process plates sterling silver with gold leaf. Vermeil has the brilliance of gold and is made both in flatware and holloware by American silver manufacturers. Its silver content makes monogramming possible.

DICTIONARY OF FOOD, FOREIGN PHRASES AND MENU TERMS

As our world becomes smaller, more and more foods from other countries will appear on menus.

This list includes terms that appear in cookbooks, magazines and newspapers. Many of them are used in restaurants and on the menus and menu cards. To know the meaning, the pronunciation and the origin whenever possible gives great confidence in ordering food. It should add much to the eating pleasure for host, hostess or guest. Many of the phrases or terms have been borrowed from the cuisine of other countries and accepted into the English language.

The abbreviations indicate the country or land of origin: A-American; E-English; F-French; G-German; I-Italian; R-Russian; S-Spanish; AG-Austrian-German; Mex.-Mexican; Scan.-Scandinavian.

After-dinner Coffee: strong black coffee served at the end of dinner usually in very small cups (demitasse) at the table or in the living room.

Ala (F) (ah la), **Au** (o, or oh), **Aux** (ō, or ōh): French phrases meaning style; prepared or served in a certain style "with" or "in," depending on use.

Ala Carte (F) (ah la cart′): selection of individual items from a restaurant menu paying for each food ordered. See Table d'hote.

Ala King: a white sauce originally created for white meat of chicken (see Chicken ala King). Today other protein-rich foods are served in this sauce and appear on menus, as eggs ala King, tuna and other sea foods, turkey ala King, etc.

Ala Mode (F) (ah la mōde): traditionally pie topped with ice cream. Cake is often served ala mode. Also an entree in the French manner as a pot roast of beef en casserole, Beef ala Mode.

Alfresco or Al fresco (S) (al frĕs kō): reference to a style of serving —in the fresh, cool air or outdoors; a luncheon Al fresco; prepared (implying an outdoor grill) and served Al fresco.

Antipasto (I) (ăn ti pas tō): a variety of Italian relishes, cheese, fish, ham, assorted olives, pickled peppers arranged on individual plates and served as a luncheon or dinner first course appetizer plate. Also served as an entree.

Au Gratin (F) (ō grá tan′): specifically referring to topping of buttered bread crumbs and grated cheese for casseroles, then baked until crispy brown. Also used as the topping over a cheese or mushroom sauce for a hearty open-face sandwich on heat proof platter for similar browning in the broiler or oven.

Au Jus (F) (ō zhōō′): served with natural juices which drain during cooking, such as Roast Beef au Jus.

Au Natural (F) (o natural): fresh or natural, such as large cherries, strawberries with stems or hull left on each piece of fruit; often accompanied by confectioners' sugar, sour cream. The fruit may be a first course at breakfast, a luncheon dessert, or a snack.

Aux Fines Herbes (F) (ō fēēnzerb): meaning with fine aromatic herbs—chervil, chives, parsley, thyme and tarragon leaves, finely chopped and added to other ingredients. For example, omelette aux Fines Herbes—the finely chopped herbs are added to egg mixture before cooking.

Beef Stroganoff (R) (beef strog′ o noff): entree of very thin slices of tenderloin, quickly sautéed, added to and served in a special sauce of consommé, mushrooms, onion, sour cream and condiments; — named after Count Paul Stroganoff, a 19th century diplomat.

Bisque (F) (bĭsk): a thick soup usually of fish with a cream sauce base.

Bouillabaisse (F) (boo yah beás): a thick soup combining a variety of sea foods.

Bouillon (F) (bool′yon or bool yoń): the brown stock from cooking beef used as base for sauces and soups. Clarified it may be served as a clear broth for a first course appetizer. (see Consommé).

Bouquet Garni (F) (bōō kāy gâr nē): a combination of selected herbs, parsley, thyme and scallions tied into a bunch and added to sauces, soups or stews.

Brochette (F) (brō shet′): skewer—for example, ala brochette meaning broiled, grilled or roasted on a skewer.

Cafe au Lait (F) (kàh fāy āh lē): hot coffee with hot milk.

Cafe Noir (F) (kah fāy nwaher): black coffee.

Canapé (F) (kăn á pā or pĭ): bite-size fried bread, crackers or toast or tiny biscuits split and toasted, spread with savory pastes (see Paté) or topped with bits of savory meat, poultry, fish or cheese.

Capers (kā pers): small greenish flower buds of a Mediterranean bush, pickled and used to flavor sauces, added to meats and poultry, meat salads, and as a garnish. (see Steak Tartare)

Carafe (F) (kȧ räf′): water bottle of glass or crystal commonly used for filling water glasses.

Carte de Jour (F) (kahrt du jo͞or): restaurant bill of fare for the day.

Cayenne (F) (kī or kā eń): a very hot red pepper condiment (see Paprika). Only a few grains are necessary to give zest to a sauce.

Chateaubriand (F) (shăh tōh brē′a): a thick slice cut from the center of the beef tenderloin, broiled or grilled over high heat to brown the surface and retain inside rareness. Considered a deluxe steak. (see Filet)

Chicken ala King: entree of diced white meat of chicken in a rich white sauce with mushrooms, bits of green pepper and pimiento and often a touch of sherry. Created by an American Chef to salute his employer, owner of King's Restaurant outside New York City in the early eighteenth century.

Consommé (F) (kŏn-sō-mā): a broth of clarified brown stock and clarified white stock, the latter prepared from cooking chicken or veal (see Bouillon).

Coq au vin (F) (kŏḱ ō văng): chicken cooked in red wine.

Cordon Bleu (F) (kôr′ doǹ blö): of "blue ribbon" distinction or quality—also the name of a French school of cookery.

Crepes Suzette (F) (crepe soo zet′): very thin, delicate pancakes rolled up, sprinkled with sugar and served with a special sauce.

Croutons (F) (croo toń): small cubes of toasted or fried bread. Often served with a soup or tossed with salad ingredients, especially with salad greens.

Cuisine (F) (kwĭ zēń): meaning style of cooking—for example, a restaurant may be a French cuisine, an Austria-American cuisine, etc.

Culinary (kŭl or kewl ĭ nahr i): pertaining to cookery or kitchen—such as culinary herbs, culinary skill.

Demitasse (F) (dem i tas): very small cup for serving strong black coffee. Also used to refer to the beverage.

Dip or **Dips** (A): modern term for the dipping or dunking mixtures—accompanied by bread sticks, crackers, potato chips, pretzels, melba toast and crisp vegetables such as cauliflower flowerettes, broccoli fingers (cut from the stalk), zucchini slices, etc. (see Fondue 2)

Entree (F) (an´ trā): meaning main dish.

Escargot (F) (es car gō′): a small edible snail, usually served in its shell.

Filet (F) (fi lā′):a boneless piece of meat or fish. (1) Filet of beef or tenderloin of beef refers to the entire piece or whole tenderloin; (2) Filet Mignon (F) (fi lā min yon′) refers to a small steak cut from the tenderloin (see Chateaubriand).

Fondue (F) (fon′ do͞o) or (fon do͞o′): Three distinctive dishes are included under Fondues.

(1) **Beef Fondue:** tenderloin of beef cut into bite-size cubes impaled on fondue fork, quickly cooked in hot oil and served with piquant sauces. Served as an appetizer or entree.

(2) **Swiss Fondue:** an appetizer or entree of melted natural cheeses in a fondue pot or chafing dish into which bite-size cubes of bread impaled on a long fork are dipped one at a time. Fresh crisp fruits and vegetables cut into suitable pieces may be included, such as apple wedges, broccoli fingers (from the peeled lower stalk), cauliflower flowerettes, carrots, celery, green pepper strips, radish and zucchini slices.

(3) **Baked Cheese Fondue:** an entree made of a custard base, grated or sliced cheese and bread cubes or slices of bread. Baked and served en casserole.

Frijoles (frē hōlz): the pinto beans of the Mexican pink or red variety; cooked in water until very tender; mashed and flavored with bacon fat or lard. May be cooked to a moist, or dry consistency; a favorite and important dish to the people of Mexico and southwestern United States.

Fruit Soup (Scan.): A soup, originally and still prepared by cooking dried fruits. The fruit is left whole. The "juice" is slightly thickened with potato starch, tapioca or sago. It is served warm or cold as a first course appetizer-soup or as a dessert. Canned, fresh or frozen fruits can also be used. Cinnamon, nutmeg, grated lemon or orange rind and a dollop of sour cream may be used for variety, according to taste and menu use.

Hors d'oeuvres (F) (ôr dovr′): meaning "outside of work;" therefore served before a meal. It is the French equivalent for appetizer. Should be small—one or two bite size and well seasoned.

Indian Pudding: a traditional New England Colonial dessert of corn meal, milk, sweetening, egg, currants or raisins, slow baked to a creamy consistency and served warm—often with a deluxe touch of ice cream.

Julienne (F) (jo͞o lĭ ĕń): cut in match-like strips, such as vegetables added to clear soup; meat, poultry, cheese and vegetables added to salad.

Macaroni (măc a ró nĭ): Macaroni products is general term and usually included with pasta (see Pasta).

Macedoine (F) (mâh sāy dwan′): mixture of fruits or vegetables.

Marinade (F) (mâr i nādé): a highly flavored seasoning liquid in which foods are "soaked" to flavor, to season and to tenderize according to recipe.

Marinate (mâŕ ĭ nāte): to season foods in a marinade for purposes given above.

Meringue (F) (mĕ răng): (1) the soft topping of egg whites, sugar, and flavoring placed on cream pies and browned in oven; (2) the hard meringue-crisp, tender, very fine mixture-of egg whites, sugar and flavoring and slow baked and used as a base for ice cream, fruit and whipped cream for a deluxe dessert.

Minestrone (I) (mĭń e strō nĭ): a hearty soup of a pasta and vegetables in a meat stock base (see Pasta below).

Mousse (F) (mo͞ose): (1) a rich dessert of whipped cream, flavoring syrups (chocolate or maple) usually molded, then hard-frozen. (2) also an entree of cooked meat or fish, finely minced, puréed or put through the blender, then mixed with a broth base, gelatin and whipped cream. Usually molded in a fancy form, then chilled thoroughly. Buffet table favorites such as chicken or turkey mousse, salmon, ham.

Paella (I) (pĕ el a): a thick "stew" of chicken, sausage, seafood, vegetables with saffron-flavored rice. A meal-in-a-pot entree.

Paprika (pà prḗ ka or păp rĭ ká): very mild red condiment ground from a dried sweet red pepper. A popular garnish sprinkled over food to add color; also added to sauces to heighten color (see Cayenne).

Parfait (F) (pahr fāy′): a special dessert of ice cream, flavoring syrup or fruit sauces, topped with whipped cream and nuts served very cold in tall, narrow, footed dessert glasses.

Pasta (I) (päs tá): term referring to noodles, spaghetti and vermicelli products in a wide variety of shapes, sizes and forms (alphabet, bow-knots, shells, etc.). Macaroni is usually included in this group; also dish of cooked pasta.

Paté (F) (pä′ tāy): well seasoned "paste," of cooked meat or chicken livers, finely mashed, or put through the blender. It is popular as an appetizer for canapés, dips, etc.

Paté de Foie Gras (F) (fwa gra): paté of fatted goose liver.

Pièce de Résistance (F) (pea yes de ray zees tahns′): entree or main dish of the meal.

Pilaf (pé läf): cooked rice in meat or chicken stock (the spelling, pronunciation and seasonings vary according to its country of origin.) Meat and/or vegetables may be cooked with the rice. Curry, saffron or thyme or oregano are all seasoning choices. Served as a meat accompaniment or an entree.

Quiche Lorraine (F) (keesh Lorraine): open-face custard pie with chopped bacon, onion and cheese. Served hot as an entree—also as an appetizer.

Restaurateur (F) (res′ ta ra tur′): individual who owns and/or manages a restaurant.

Sauerbraten (A-G) (sauer braten): pot roast of beef marinated in vinegar, herbs, spices and onion before cooking (braising).

Sherbet (shur′ bet): a frozen light water ice with piquant fruit flavor such as lemon, orange or raspberry; often beaten egg white is added during freezing to give additional lightness.

Soufflé (F) (soo flay′): (1) hot entree of fish, meat, poultry and/or vegetables combined with a sauce and of a characteristic puffy lightness from added beaten egg whites; (2) also a dessert such as chocolate, lemon, orange with the same qualities of lightness from added beaten egg whites.

Steak Tartare (popularly called steak cannibal style): an entree sandwich of raw, chopped or ground round steak seasoned with salt, pepper, minced onion, horseradish, and one raw egg for each serving, then formed into a loose flat cake and served on chilled plate. Garnished with minced parsley and a few capers. Served with French or rye bread. May be served as an open-sandwich, on hot toast; also a popular buffet entree served in a large bowl surrounded with condiments and breadstuffs.

Strudel (A-G) (strōō d′l): a dessert made of a very special dough, stretched to transparent thinness, layered with sliced apples, raisins, almonds, cinnamon and sugar, rolled up to form a long roll and baked. It is usually sprinkled with confectioners' sugar before serving.

Table d'hote (F) (tah blĭ dōté): menu term meaning a complete meal of any number of courses. Cost of the complete meal depends upon entree selection.

Tempura (tĕm poo ra): an oriental entree—small pieces of boneless meat or poultry, vegetables, batter-dipped and deep-fat fried, served hot with variations of soy sauces; may also be served as a hot appetizer.

SUGGESTED READINGS

"Definitions of Processes in Food Preparation," *Handbook of Food Preparation,* XV, Washington, D.C.: American Home Economics Association, 1959, pp. 47-48.

Fashions in Dining. Hidden Value Series. Chicago: Sears, Roebuck & Co., Consumer Information Division.

Glassware Today. New York: American Glassware Association.

Vanderbilt, Amy. *Amy Vanderbilt's New Complete Book of Etiquette.* Garden City: Doubleday and Co., Inc., 1963.

Webster's Third New International Dictionary of the English Language. Unabridged. Springfield, Mass.: B & C Merriam Co.